STORIED LEADERSHIP

STORIED LEADERSHIP

Foundations of Leadership from a Christian Perspective

Brian Jensen
Keith R Martel

Foreward by Donald Opitz, PhD

Falls City Press
Beaver Falls, Pennsylvania

STORIED LEADERSHIP
Foundations of Leadership from a Christian Perspective

© 2015 Falls City Press

Published by Falls City Press
2108 Seventh Avenue
Beaver Falls, PA 15010
www.fallscitypress.com

Printed in the United States of America

Scripture quotations are from the English Standard Version unless otherwise indicated.

The Holy Bible, English Standard Version® (ESV®)
Copyright © 2001 by Crossway,
a publishing ministry of Good News Publishers.
All rights reserved

Some names and identifying characteristics in this book have been
changed to protect the privacy of those represented.

Publisher's Cataloging-in-Publication Data

Jensen, Brian, 1980-
Martel, Keith R, 1975-
    Storied leadership : foundations of leadership from a Christian
    perspective / by Brian Jensen and Keith R. Martel.
        p. cm.
    Includes bibliographical references and index.
    ISBN: 978-0-9864051-0-5 (paper)
    ISBN: 978-0-9864051-2-9 (e-book)

1. Christian leadership   I. Title
BV 4597.53.L43.J36 2015   248.411   2015930481

2 4 6 8 10 9 7 5 3 1

To Kristie and Sara,
for enriching our stories.

CONTENTS

Foreward

I grew up in the trees—not as a monkey or in a tree house but with trees all around. My parents were both teachers, and that opened up summers for camping among trees beside a small pond. It wasn't paradise, but in my memory all these years later, it was. This book isn't about trees, but it isn't really about leadership either. These two authors, both former grad students of mine and now (I'm so pleased to say) dear friends, are not botanists. And they are not attempting a scientific analysis or a diagnostic biopsy of leadership. They have stepped back from the trees in order to see the forest.

Like me these authors are weary of books that turn leadership into a technique or a program. They recognize that leadership is not a form of coercion or a mode of control; rather it is a relationship. It is a pattern of social life and that pattern emerges in a narrative context. Leadership always takes place as part of a story of human interaction, a story of human culture, and it takes place within the local forest of need, opportunity, obstacle, and vision. This book addresses the wide web of life, human and creational contexts, the God-governed historical context too, in which leadership always takes place.

Seeing the big picture is the heart of biblical wisdom. Again and again the wisdom literature asks, where are you? The wise guys of the bible answer, "in the creation-house of the Lord." And the text asks, who are you? The wise guys answer, "we are guests in the great house and in the forested playfields of the Gracious Host."

Keith and Brian are wise guys, and they are asking us to step back to see the big picture. My hope for this book isn't simply that it fosters 10,000 conversations about leadership, but that it models for us all a way of seeing and living. Perhaps after reading it we will pause, step back, and reflect about life, place and meaning, and in doing this we'll find ourselves reflecting upon the deep source of each—the Lord of Life, the King of the Kingdom, and the Word of Truth. We are all invited into this story. If you step in, you'll find that you've been cast a character in this epic story of stewardship, love, and yes, leadership.

Donald Opitz, PhD
Messiah College, Chaplain
Co-Author of
Learning for the Love of God

Acknowledgments

I n his book *Steal Like an Artist*, Austin Kleon writes, "You are, in fact, a mashup of what you choose to let into your life."[1] Kleon's words are indicative of this project and our lives. We begin these acknowledgments admitting that nothing we have ever written is truly our own. We are standing on the shoulders of giants. Or, as the proverb teaches us, there is nothing new under the sun. This work is a conglomeration, reconfiguration, and reinvention of the ideas we have read, heard, talked about, and wandered through over the past several decades.

The words of authors in and around the reformational perspective have marked our understanding of and practices in the world. Authors Brian Walsh, Al Wolters, Jamie Smith, Andy Crouch, Nicholas Wolterstorff, Richard Mouw, Amy Sherman, Richard Middleton, and Calvin Seerveld have affected us from afar. Their books are heavily marked, tattered, and dog-eared from years of perusal. We have both been deeply moved by many mentors. Chief amongst these are Steve Garber, Brad Frey, and Don Opitz. Each of them, in different ways, have been with us through the journey in a world of gravity and grace.

There is also the membership of Geneva College and our local congregations. We are grateful for the women and men who have nurtured us and taught with us in the classroom (in the Humanities and the Masters in Higher Education programs) and beyond in the work of Student Development. Also, of course, are the many students who have inspired and encouraged our work along the way.

We are both grateful for the influence of the CCO (Coalition for Christian Outreach) and the important work they do in the lives of college students. We are different people because of this organization. The CCO's Jubilee conference is perhaps the most important gathering of young people in America. For decades it has helped students understand the connection between the grand biblical story and their lives and vocations. Through our relationships with the CCO we have fallen in love with the work of Byron and Beth Borger in their little corner of the Kingdom, as owners of Hearts & Minds Books. They are wise companions in our storied lives. Thanks to Byron for a final careful reading.

We are deeply indebted to our Beta Readers who took the time to wade through a first "final draft." They provided push back, encouragement, and humor to the process. For making time to read and respond we would like to thank: Jonathan Bacon, Krista Barnett, Sara Bauer, Chelsi Cannon, Nick Carson, Joel Comanda, Tim Edris, Anjelica Farino, Cliff Kelly, David Ketter, David Opalka, Anne Patterson, Jana Postma, Chris Stern, Tori Trapanick, and Greg Veltman. We must give a special thanks to our Alpha Beta reader, Jason Panella, who sweated over our words and gave us something a bit more beautiful and David Opalka who waved his design wand over our cover art in an act of restoration.

Of course, there are friends and colleagues, too many to name, who have contributed to our development in the ways we learn, love, live, and lead. All of these are important members of the mashup. Particular thanks to Scott Calgaro for listening, asking, and offering some answers and Patrick Boyle for being the quintessential example of creation and restoration.

Most of our gratitude ought to go to our wives and kids. They have been supportive and patient. All of the stories about them in these pages are mostly true.

Finally, thanks be to the Lord of creation and restoration. We are grateful to have been drawn into His story, by His grace, and given a part to play.

Soli Deo gloria.

Introduction

Snow slowly drifted through the crisp night sky, an early harbinger of the tough-as-steel winter that would soon be upon western Pennsylvania. As usual, we chatted about the many aspects of our lives. We lingered on the state of our marriages and shared ridiculous stories about our kids. Our conversation—as it often does—meandered toward working with students in the classrooms and hallways of our small Christian college.

Having worked in higher education for all of our professional lives, we have sifted through resources available for our leaders to aid them in understanding their role as influencers in the world. Bookstore shelves are lined with texts offering tricks of the trade, steps to successful leading, and management techniques. Although many books utilize passages of Scripture to reinforce their methods for Christian leaders, there remains a space on the shelf for a book that asks more fundamental questions about the nature of reality—a book that investigates the foundations of leadership from a Christian perspective.

Over the years, we created a patchwork of resources by various authors, yet we still had not come up with the resource we were looking for. On that night we committed to write the book that we had always hoped to share, read, and discuss with leaders on our campus. We are delighted that you have decided to join our journey and engage in this conversation.

Consider for a moment the impressive skyline of Manhattan. Many have studied how it is possible to build massive skyscrapers, some of the biggest in the world, on an island. Most islands of its size could not sustain these massive structures. Daniel Muhlenburg explains:

> Manhattan's skyline was made possible by two things: Henry Bessemer's advent of the Bessemer Process in 1858 that allowed for the mass production of steel, and the bedrock that the island rests on. The latter is important because without Manhattan's unique geological foundation...no skyscrapers could have ever risen on the island. You can't build skyscrapers in someplace like, say, Long Island, where no bedrock exists and the ground is too soft to support the weight of tall buildings. In short, no bedrock, no skyline.[1]

The evolution of new technologies was pivotal in the creation of the Big Apple's skyscrapers, but all of the processes would be useless without the solid foundation of Manhattan's bedrock. The bedrock made the buildings possible. In many ways, the discourse surrounding leadership proceeds like a construction team erecting a skyscraper without knowing exactly what lies below the surface. We contend that the assumptions held about reality are the ultimate foundation of one's perspective on leadership. One's final assumptions about the nature of things—or worldview— not only hold up his or her perspective on leadership, but also serve as a powerful shaping force.

There is a pressing need for gifted and committed leaders in our society. However, to lead well requires a solid foundational perspective. Our purpose is to consider leadership from a Christian perspective by first digging below the surface. The biblical narrative, developed through the entirety of the scriptures, helps us to understand the nature of the world, who we are in the world, and where reality is heading. This storied perspective provides a solid groundwork from which to discover the particular call to leadership, what leadership is, and how we—as people in the story—ought to lead.

Recent decades have seen an influx of leadership resources. This period comes on the heels of a century's worth of investigation into the meaning of leadership. This work produced significant research and helpful theories. Leadership is truly a complex subject. Ralph Stogdill writes, "There are almost as many definitions of leadership as there are persons who have attempted to define the concept."[2] It is often difficult to wrap our minds around this multidimensional topic, but leadership scholars have attempted to do just that for decades. *Storied Leadership* is meant to develop a foundation capable of contributing to the ever-expanding exploration into the world of leadership.

Prior to the mid-1970s, leadership models still operated out of what was referred to as the "industrial paradigm." It was commonplace to use management and leadership synonymously, assuming that quality leadership was simply good management. This included an approach that valorized progress and efficiency. Getting things done was the name of the game. Leaders were defined primarily as those who had specific traits and displayed particular behaviors suited for accomplishing certain ends. The "Great Man Theory" of the early 20th century was especially influential for the world of leadership.

This theory characterized a leader by identifying traits like charisma, power, and intelligence. A person was simply born a leader. Leadership was a particularly western-informed and male-dominated arena. The elemental problem with this paradigm is not that it is built out of bad techniques, but rather that is birthed from faulty assumptions about reality. It emerges from a defective foundation. The field of leadership has come a long way over the past century; however, you will still encounter many authors attempting to explain leadership through formulas. These are the incomplete mindsets and theories that we have struggled with while searching for resources to use with our young leaders.

Before commencing, there are a few things will aid in your reading. Since traditional notions of leadership have been ingrained in us for years, these initial comments should serve in cleansing your palette of some common assumptions. First, Christ-like living ought to permeate *all* contexts and call us to faithfulness in *all* areas of our lives. This is important as we consider our leadership. Leading is not separate from, or merely part of, our lives. Rather, it is intentionally integrated as we practice multifaceted faithful service in the Kingdom of God.

Second, we are undeniably servants. Embedded in the life of discipleship is the call to service. This cannot be compartmentalized. It is an integral part of our lives. From this posture of servanthood we then lead. At times with official titles, but more often within unlabeled positions of influence. Regardless of the situation, we lead and we follow as servants of our Lord, Jesus Christ.

Third, we will define leadership as a *collaborative effort that influences positive purposeful changes*. As Christians, called to a life of faithfulness and restoration, leadership is a calling placed on each of us. Through a Kingdom perspective, we see leadership as an inescapable vocation for the Christian life. It is an act of collaboration not only because of efficacy, but also because of our design. We were created as communal beings that work best as members of a unified whole.

Fourth, we question the assumption that leadership only concerns people who hold particular positions of power. Many assume that there are leaders and there are followers; leaders lead and followers follow. *Leadership* is more complex than a leader/follower duality. We agree with Joseph Rost as he moves to reconfigure the leadership framework, "Followers do not do followership, they do leadership. Both leaders and followers form one relationship that is leadership." He continues, "[Leaders and followers] do not do the same thing in the relationship...but they are both essential to leadership."[3] Throughout the narrative of the scriptures, God's people are called together into an active role of developing and restoring of His world, that is, positive purposeful change.

This is a book about storied leadership. We believe that a conception of leadership from a Christian perspective must emerge from the narrative of the scriptures. This book proceeds by way of two sections. The first is devoted to exploring the story of the scriptures and configuring how a perspective on reality emerges from this story. We are suggesting that all living and leading emerges from a person's (and their community's) fundamental assumptions about reality. What we believe about the nature of the world, and the role of humans in it, will always shape our posture toward, and behavior in, the world. We will explain how these assumptions always emerge from stories we believe and tell about reality. Further, we are fully committed to the fact that every leadership model and all acts of leading are manifestations of the stories that we believe. Although we hold that these chapters contain much that is "useful," it is primarily a consideration of the story of the scriptures and the shaping power it has on our perspectives concerning life and leadership. This section is initiated with an explanation of the influence and place of narrative and proceeds into the story of the Bible. We then work to develop the ramifications of the story and the roles as well as the purposes of leadership that surface from it.

The second section is intended to give clear and helpful practices that are based on the fundamental principles in section one—practical manifestations of the foundation discussed. We hope that readers will find these short chapters helpful in understanding and discussing leadership on at work, in their churches, and throughout their communities.

Finally, although *Storied Leadership* can be read and reflected on alone, we have created it to be a collaborative effort. Our hope is that you will read this with friends, mentors, or co-workers. At the end of each chapter, there is a list of questions for reflection and discussion. If used well, we expect these to help you further engage the story and discuss its implications.

We also invite you to reflect on social media. Tweet it, post it, Instagram it. We hope this becomes a broad conversation!

We would love to hear your thoughts:

On Twitter: @StoriedLeader or @krmartel
Via Email: storiedleadership@fallscitypress.com

Now, let's begin the adventure of Storied Leadership

CHAPTER 1
Storied Leadership

O ne afternoon I walked in on my daughter having an existential crisis. Simone's big beautiful eyes beamed through her plastic bedazzled glasses. "Dad, what's it all for anyway? We go to work, go to school, make money, buy stuff, go to sleep, get up, go to work, eat dinner, go to school, have kids, go to sleep, get up..." Nearly in tears, she went on. I was taken aback. I expected these kinds of questions, but I did not imagine her asking them before finishing the second grade.

My wife and I had always hoped for inquisitive kids. There Simone was, standing with curled-up toes on the cold ceramic tile, asking the same big questions I explore with emerging adults in the laid-back cafés and classrooms of the college campus. Although my wife and I were surprised, we shouldn't have been. For years we endeavored to shape a home life that encourages curiosity and awe in the face of a grand world. But on that day, the curiosity led her to difficult questions. Her seven-year old words echoed the ancient opening of Ecclesiastes:

Vanity of vanities, says the Preacher,
vanity of vanities! All is vanity.
What does man gain by all the toil
at which he toils under the sun?
A generation goes, and a generation comes,
but the earth remains forever.
The sun rises, and the sun goes down,
and hastens to the place where it rises.
The wind blows to the south
and goes around to the north;
around and around goes the wind,
and on its circuits the wind returns.
All streams run to the sea,
but the sea is not full;
to the place where the streams flow,
there they flow again.
All things are full of weariness;
a man cannot utter it;
the eye is not satisfied with seeing,
nor the ear filled with hearing.
What has been is what will be,
and what has been done is what will be done,
and there is nothing new under the sun.
(Ecclesiastes 1:2-9)

These words have spoken to the human experience for
millennia. Considering Ecclesiastes, novelist and play-
wright Thomas Wolfe writes, "Of all I have ever seen or
learned, that book seems to me the noblest, the wisest,
and the most powerful expression of man's life upon
this earth."[1]

It is telling that old playwrights, poets, seven-year-
olds, college students, and pastors come to the same

questions, isn't it? There is something so universal and *human* about these queries. How do we make sense of a world that doesn't always seem coherent? How do we find meaning when, at times, being in the world feels like running on an eternally spinning treadmill? What is it all for anyway? How do we lead others who are also asking these questions?

Philosophers, theologians, artists, students, and yes, even dads have toiled to answer these questions for themselves and for those whom they try to lead. However, we do not ask these questions in isolation. Communities consider them together and search for answers within a context of interpretation. That is, they look at the world and ultimately tell stories about the nature of reality. They find themselves in groups that make very local decisions about the most important questions: What does it mean to be human? Why aren't things the way they should be? What is valuable? What is the reason for being? Asking is part of being human and it is a fundamentally communal experience.

Although nearly two decades separates both Simone from my students and my students from me, our fundamental questions remain eerily similar. The approach to finding answers to these cosmic questions is much the same for all of us. As my wife and I navigate the labyrinth of kid curiosity and student wonder, we find that most answers lie in the stories we believe and tell about reality. Brian Walsh and Steven Bauma-Prediger, authors of *Beyond Homelessness*, write, "This is a very important point: human life is narratively rooted."[2] As humans, on a very tacit level, we know the power of stories. Stories are all around us. They have the ability to inspire and

madden, to illicit suspense and relief. The politically savvy
can assuage a crowd more successfully with a story than a
ten-point plan. Stories of trials and hope can comfort us
in our own times of trouble. Stories can paint a picture of
a flourishing life.

WHAT'S IN A STORY?

What does it mean that stories shape reality? They are
descriptions of the state of things. They can also cast a
picture of a better world and how it might come to be. In
The Drama of Scripture, Craig Bartholomew and Michael
Goheen explain it this way:

> In order to understand our world, to make sense of
> our lives, and to make our most important decisions
> about how we ought to be living, we depend upon
> story. In fact, among some philosophers, theolo-
> gians, and biblical scholars, there is a growing rec-
> ognition that 'a story...is...the best way of talking
> about how the world actually is.'[3]

Their point is evident when we think of the most profound
teachers and pastors. While they can adeptly explain concepts in accessible ways, the best of them tell stories that
make abstract ideas concrete.

Understanding stories about reality in this way, we can
begin to realize their power. A well-crafted story can transform our conception of reality. In fact, there is a movement
in the field of psychotherapy aptly named "narrative therapy." These practitioners muster the power of story as they
move hurting people towards healing and restoration. Para-
mount to narrative therapy is the consideration that people

have been told and retold big stories about reality that are damaging and even damning. Narrative therapists guide their patients in reflecting on these dominant stories. The patient recognizes that their story has been constructed by another, and that aspects of this story are false.

Thinkers throughout the ages have reminded us that "ideas have legs." This is true. The best teachers are not only able to explain an idea, but then also articulate it in the context of story in such a way that the concept comes to life. Narratives can also humanize ideas. As a first year political science student, I made fast friends with John, another young and eager student. We had long conversations about the state of welfare in our nation.

At eighteen, John could make cohesive arguments against the institution of a strong welfare system. A few years into college his sister fell on hard times through a broken relationship that led to her living on the margins and struggling to make it in a difficult world with a newborn baby. John's sister found much-needed relief through aspects of the welfare system that my friend had so ardently argued against. Encountering the story of his sister, John's theoretical position could no longer stand in abstraction. It all became very real. It forced him to reconsider his position.

Stories, however, are not just ways of *knowing* the world. Western culture, especially within the halls of academia, is haunted by the ghost of 17th century philosopher René Descartes. That is, we have come to believe that human beings are primarily *res cogito*—cognitive beings. Contrary to this, professor and author James K.A. Smith explains that humans are "embodied actors, not just thinking things."[4]

A major aspect of the power of stories is how they can move the way we feel. They also shape what we love.

Smith adeptly considers story and the human condition. He writes, "Our hearts traffic in stories. Not only are we lovers, we are storytellers—and story-listeners." He continues, "We are narrative animals whose very orientation to the world is fundamentally shaped by stories."[5] This should be no surprise. Reflecting on our favorite stories—whether films, novels, songs, or family lore—we realize that we love them, not primarily because of how they make us think (in a theoretical way), but more so because of the way they make us feel. Reading Cormac McCarthy's *The Road*, we *feel* the dedication of a father to his son as they travel in the post-apocalyptic wasteland, *Romeo and Juliet* makes us *long* for fulfilling love, the devastated creation depicted in *Wall-E* can deeply *convict* us of our own abuses of God's creation, *The Dark Knight inspires* us to be superhuman in the face of injustice, and Eminem's "Lose Yourself" *stirs* in us courage to overcome disabling fear.

It only takes a few minutes watching the flickering images on the television screen before we encounter the stories masterfully crafted by advertising agencies. Perhaps no one knows the power of narrative as well as these shepherds of the human heart. In as little as thirty-seconds, the best ad agencies are able to tell a story that reshapes our desires and directs our longings toward their products. The industry knows that the fastest way to a human's wallet is not through the brain, but through the heart. Creating a story of a better world, the best advertisers clearly and concisely tell a story about a better way of being—a potential means of human flourishing that always includes their product. Corporate taglines, from

Apple's "Think Different," to Burger King's "Your Way, Right Away," don't just tell us something, they make us feel.

HOW STORIES WORK

While dominant stories about reality are powerful, the human heart is not so easily captured. I do not feel the need to buy an F-150 because I heard Denis Leary's voice-over on a commercial one time. This is why Ford airs the same commercial over and over (*ad nauseum*) during a single football game. It is the telling and retelling of a story that allows it to set in—to seep into our marrow.

We tell and retell stories because the repetition has a way of working the story into our hearts.

This is also why my church repeatedly reads the scriptures together and why before we fall asleep, no matter what, I tell my wife that I love her.

One of my favorite Old Testament stories is in the beginning of the book of Joshua. It depicts the people of Israel crossing the Jordan into the Promised Land. God commands something peculiar of them. He tells them to take twelve large rocks, one for each tribe, and make a pillar. Then He tells them:

> When your children ask in time to come, "What do those stones mean to you?" then you shall tell them that the waters of the Jordan were cut off before the ark of the covenant of the LORD. When it passed over the Jordan, the waters of the Jordan were cut off. So these stones shall be to the people of Israel a memorial forever. (Joshua 4:6-7)

Do you see what He did there? The storytelling God sets up a catalyst to transform forgetful people into those who remember. When the children ask, "What's with that big pile of rocks anyway?" The elders were to tell the story, over and over again. The narrative of the provision of God would become ingrained through storytelling. This is one of many examples in the scriptures of the power of repeating the story.

Another key characteristic of stories is that they are temporal—they deal with the past, the present, and the future. This is simple yet profound. We often think of stories primarily in terms of the past. The scriptures seem to tell the story of a people from long ago. Naturally, this is so. Stories about reality are also powerful in the way they inform our present situation in the world. The recounting of the stories of the past informs the present: who we are, where we are, what we are to do, and why the world is this way.

Nevertheless, stories virtually always deal with the future as well. We all know the narrative trope "happily ever after" or an image of the hero riding off into the sunset. Although these devices are used to pull a story together, to give the current narrative a sense of closure, a good closing scene often drives the story into the future. The ever-after tells us that no story really ends, but even in its conclusion, the story maintains a future horizon. Be it Marx, Vonnegut, Rawling, or Dostoyevsky, the best authors paint a picture of these horizons. Likewise, the stories we tell about reality also point toward the future.

Being a Gen-Xer I grew up throughout the tail end of the Cold War. My memories of this time are vivid. My childhood story about reality was always influenced by the arms race and what was then called Mutual Assured Destruction. As the United States and the U.S.S.R. stared each other down, both nations amassed so many nuclear warheads that if either initiated an attack a massive volley of missiles would ensue. I had images of launch codes and mushroom clouds embedded in my dreams and imagination. For those born after the Cold War, this might sound ludicrous, but I was nearly positive that the entire world was going to come to an end through nuclear war and the complete devastation of all things.

More recently, in the years leading up to the recent economic crash of 2008, there was a story that our nation came to trust about the housing market. From 1997 to 2006, American houses increased in value at a national average of 124%. As the housing market soared, people believed that the current conditions would necessarily continue into the future. The story of the past shaped the narrative of the future. Imagine how this story would affect those living within it. "Knowing" that their houses would be worth more, people borrowed against their homes to finance everything from widescreen TVs to their children's college tuition.

Prospective home buyers were given sub-prime mortgages with dangerous adjustable rates that would go up astronomically after the first five years. These loans were signed because people "knew" that as their homes inevitably increased in value they would be able to refinance them for better, safer contracts. We now know that the housing market did not continue to increase in value. The bubble burst and the market crashed. This is a perfect example of making decisions in the present based on stories about the past that shape narratives of the future. And this one resulted in severe consequences.

A final peculiar characteristic of stories is that they are not, for the most part, on the forefront of our minds. They do not run like a film reel before us as we navigate the world. Most often, they operate in the background. Even when we do not explicitly think about them, narratives are ever-present. We believe a story about the world and operate according to it, even if we do not know it exists.

Recently, I led a class of graduate students to Rome to study Italian higher education. Throughout the course, students were amazed by the differences not only between the educational systems, but also our cultures. One Italian student we met told us that it is common for people to live with their parents until they are between twenty-eight and thirty-two years old—only to leave when they get married. This was shocking to my students. Some of them had never considered familial norms as part of the story they held about reality. For them, moving out of the home after high school (or maybe college) was simply the way things were supposed to be. This aspect of the middle-class American narrative was not held in an explicitly self-conscious way. Rather, it worked behind the scenes, shaping their expectations for life.

STORIED LEADERSHIP
Stories have everything to do with leadership. As mentioned above, our beliefs about the world take the shape of a grand narrative. Our communities, experiences, religious convictions, and interactions with great texts (books, film,

music, etc.) shape the stories we believe. All narratives are embedded with certain assumptions about the limits and possibilities of humans, the problems of the world and what creates them, and possible solutions to these problems. People always lead and influence others—for good and for ill—out of the stories that have captured their hearts and shaped their commitments.

Great stories fill our culture. Many of them are about the pain and struggle that are indicative of the human experience. They often offer ways to deal with the hurt of the world. Many of these stories are quite old and timeless; others are new and timely.

Good Will Hunting is a movie that has particularly moved my friends and me. The screenplay was written by Matt Damon and Ben Affleck soon after their own college graduation. It is about a brilliant, yet marginalized, orphan named Will Hunting. Abused and abandoned as a child, Will is a genius living a double life. In one world, he hangs out with his rough, blue collar, childhood friends—drinking, cursing, fighting, and, of course, chasing women. When we meet Will he is a janitor at the prestigious Massachusetts Institute of Technology. Will speed reads great works of literature, memorizes tort law, and solves the most vexing mathematical riddles imaginable.

As a result of a run-in with the law, Will finds himself at once under the academic tutelage of a brilliant MIT professor, Gerald Lambeau, and the care of Sean Maguire, a therapist and faculty member at Bunker Hill Community College. Will's mentors are old college roommates who chose different paths. Gerald dedicated his life to his discipline and rose to be an esteemed Fields Medal winner in mathematics. He is a rock star of the math world with adoring young disciples and swooning co-eds always at his side. Sean is a man who devoted a portion of his life to his wife's long, slow, and painful death from cancer. With wit and wisdom (and with more mental capacity than his old roommate), he teaches underprivileged college students about the fundamentals of psychology. Sean is world-weary and worn thin by grief over the loss of his true love.

Gerald and Sean, with similar capacities and educations, chose dissimilar directions because they believed different stories about reality. Both of them are trying to lead Will. Competing fundamental beliefs about reality guide their hopes for him. Gerald, seeing the brilliance of the young genius, will do anything to get Will to embrace the calling of a mathematician in the classroom, a cutting edge researcher, or even a Nobel Laureate. Sean, also abused as a child, hopes to lead Will into a place of healing from his past so that he can live more fully and authentically in the present. He desires to see his new patient learn to trust, hope, and risk. Gerald challenges and pushes, Sean laughs and listens. As a viewer, one gets the sense that both truly do care. Yet, they are leading through different means and toward different ends. This is because Sean and Gerald have divergent narratives about reality due to their backgrounds, experiences, and perspectives.

Good Will Hunting is a touching story of love and leadership. Will encounters two influencers that want the best for him. They hope to see him flourish. Each of them gives of themselves because they see the potential of a young man who can't imagine an alternative future to the dominant narrative he believes. They want to challenge Will's story. And it is the same for us.

Stories always shape our leadership. They shape who we lead, how we lead, and our consideration of what we lead others toward.

Of course, the film is also a story of pursuit. *Good Will Hunting*. The title is instructive. Naturally, it is about a misunderstood boy who, from a long life of abuse and abandonment, cannot make sense of the world. His rough exterior hides the goodness that lies within him. It is also about the search for "good will"—and the main protagonist is not the only one on the prowl. You could say it is a small story of people hunting the grand narrative. It is about people from different classes, different communities, different levels of position and power searching for what is the good will.

LEADING A STORIED PEOPLE

The chapter opened with some poignant questions posed by a curious seven-year-old. Simone's queries stood out to me because they were not technical questions. They weren't about what something is or how to do something—they had nothing to do with technique or information. Instead, she was asking fundamental question about *meaning*. To start thinking about being a person with influence, or one who leads, the most important place to begin is with "meaning" questions.

> » What does it mean to be human?

> » What does it mean to live a good life?

> » What does it mean to be in a place that experiences great anguish and also profound beauty?

> » What does it mean to be a part of "positive change"?

> » What does it mean to lead?

A narrative—with its characters, plot, setting, conflict, and resolution—answers these fundamental questions that attempt to make sense of human existence in the world. A narrative makes meaning of all that is around us. It is the bedrock on which we build our practices, from which we influence and lead.

This hunt for meaning is not new. In philosophy, from the pre-Socratics to the medievalists to the existentialists, we find passionate and even desperate pursuits of understanding the world. It is not just for the scholarly, but it is the hunt that we are all on: making meaning of what we have experienced in the past, what we perceive in the present, and what we move toward into the future. To consider leadership, we must have a foundational story that answers fundamental questions.

Is there a story that does just this?

FOR DISCUSSION OR REFLECTION:

1. What are some of your favorite stories? What makes them so captivating?

2. What are some stories of our time (in fiction or real life) that do not seem to accurately depict the world? Can you discern what they convey about reality?

3. Consider significant cultural stories about leadership. Can you determine what makes these narratives compelling?

CHAPTER 2
The Story

Growing up, my family attended a Congregationalist church in a small sleepy town on the south shore of Massachusetts. For many in my tiny town this church was the weekly gathering spot—a place for social interaction and to catch up on community gossip. Halfway through the service the kids were dismissed to Sunday school. Many weeks I turned right when others turned left. I hid in the family car to listen to Casey Casum's "Weekly Top Forty" countdown. Other times I would dutifully proceed to a classroom to hear a Bible story. I remember listening to these and thinking of them as tall tales: a man caught in the belly of a whale, three friends thrown into a furnace, and a man with a strange multi-colored jacket. I thought of the stories as fantasy. They were lore and myth. However, they also stood as stories that were indicative of lessons for children. Each stood on their own and by their own merit—cataloged in the big anthology called the Bible.

Some of these stories stayed with me. They were lessons about always telling the truth or bravely standing up for what you believe (dare to be a Daniel). Given the choice in high school, I stopped going to church and stopped hearing these stories. Through the twists and turns of adolescence, I ended up at a small Christian college in the Beaver River Valley of western Pennsylvania. In that place, I would come to hear these stories again, but this time in a very different way. Through required courses, in small group Bible studies, by way of professors and mentors, and in some of the books that landed in my hands, I learned that each of these stories that were once taught to me as standing alone and for their own devices, were actually all part of a larger narrative. Each of them a part of a master-story. The stories made more sense within the greater landscape. Synthesized, they crafted meaning for a world that seemed to have little cohesion.

There are different scholarly perspectives on the writing of the first five books of the Bible (known as the Pentateuch). Some believe they were written by Moses to the people of Israel during their time of wandering in the wilderness. Others assert that they were written for the community displaced during exile. Regardless of the perspective, you can imagine the telling of the story. A people in a state of turmoil would have been asking many of the same questions that my daughter, Will Hunting, and many of us pose: Who are we? What is the nature of this world in which we live? Why do things in this world not seem to be the way they ought to be? How are we to live? What is the good life? God's people, millennia ago, asked questions about the meaning of being in the world.

All of life is storied, including perspectives on leadership. Our understanding about the world shapes what we believe leadership is, how it ought to work, and what we are leading toward. We take time to draw out the story of the scriptures because we are convinced that without first developing a sketch of the biblical narrative we are destined to fail in developing a rich and robust vision for leadership from a Christian perspective.

IN THE BEGINNING

"Once upon a time..." is the beginning of many great fairy tales. It is an age-old opener called a "story starting phrase." It swings wide the gate of possibility—creating a horizon for a narrative to unfold. Nearly every culture has a form of "once upon a time," from the Faroese to the Luxembourgish. For the Dane, Hans Christian Andersen, it is *der var engang* and *es war einmal* for the German-speaking Brothers Grimm. Some chart the story starting phrase back to the 14th century.

The biblical story begins in a similar fashion. Someone, at some time, started a Spirit-inspired oral history that would be told and retold in an attempt to answer these primordial questions. They looked to a questioning people and said: "In the beginning God created the heavens and the earth." So begins the adventure of the biblical story.

The first three chapters of Genesis are teeming with the quintessential elements of the Christian narrative. While we cannot go into all of the details of this creation story here, there are several things that require our attention as we consider the grand narrative. First, we find God creating everything out of nothing. The scriptures tell us that He did this by His Word. God spoke the creation into being. He first says: "Let there be light. And there was light" (Genesis 1:3). Creation by God speaking is repeated time and time again: Let there be light, let there be birds, let there be, let there be, let there be. When the God who pre-existed all things spoke, the creation came into being. It had no choice. In fact, as we look throughout the scripture we can find that there is an imperative structure of the word spoken. God creates by His word, by His command, or by His law. This law throughout the creation story is a compelling law: the creation had no choice but to obey. God spoke and the universe was compelled to be. As the Psalmist tells us, the event of the creation coming into existence is a true act of its worship unto the Creator: "Let them praise the name of the LORD! For he commanded and they were created" (Psalm 148:5).

As the narrative progresses, several things are accentuated through the repetitive structure of the story. Like most good stories, there is a return to aid in the hearing and remembering of the key components of the text. The reader is told that nearly every part of the creation is "created according to their kind." A fascinating line that, if we are not careful, we could pass over with little consideration (as I did for years). "Kindedness" is of the utmost importance. Everything God made was crafted with deep intentionality. Everything was made as it ought to be. Or to put it another way, God's commanding words: "Let there be..." is a compelling command—a law. So, each thing is created according to a law structure.

Dutch attorney, philosopher, and Professor Herman Dooyeweerd—a thinker who has influenced us and many in our community—calls this the "cosmonomic idea."[1] He asserts that all things in the cosmos are created according to a *nomos*—a law. Altogether, this makes up the normative structure of reality.

All of reality has a way it ought to be.

To be made "according to their kind" means that they are not made according to another kind. A tree is not an amoeba. A lake is not a human. A bird is not a piece of fruit. It's so simple, yet deeply profound. To be made "according to their kind" means that things have certain possibilities built into them. An acorn has the potential to grow into an enormous oak tree. It can be harvested and used to build a beautiful bookcase. However, each of these also has distinct limitations. A tree cannot write poetry. God's creating word, His manifesting *nomos*, governs all that a thing is and all that it can become. At the same time, it governs that which it cannot. Everything has limits or boundaries and possibilities or potential.

The story tells us that at the end of every day "God saw all that he made and it was good." God speaks. The creation becomes, and it is good. The goodness of each thing is in its expression of its "kindedness." On the sixth day we finally find the creation of humans. In the first two chapters, we find out something about the humans' kindedness. "God said, 'let us make man in our image'..." (Genesis 1:27). *Imago Dei.* This is a fabulous and fascinating term. It is the ultimate Judeo-Christian answer to the question of the meaning of being human.

I find this term volleyed about in the chambers of my humanities courses. When I ask what it means to be human, the dutiful Christian college student answers: "To be made in the image of God." If I inquire about what exactly this means, I am often met with blank stares. There are clues in the first two chapters of Genesis that suggest the term's meaning. First, like God the Creator, we are commanded to be fruitful and fill the earth which is given to us.

Second, we are instructed to care for the creation and cultivate it. In the first creation account the humans are commanded to have "dominion" over the earth. Hearing the word dominion, we might first think that we are meant "to dominate" in a way that subjugates the creation, bending it to our desires. However, this is far from the case.

"Dominion" is derived from the Latin root *dominus*, which means Lord. You see, the creator God (our Lord) tells the created man and woman to be lords of creation. This lordship is anything but one that subjugates. It is lordship in the best way possible. A loving lord does not suppress, and she never exploits. The loving lord is the one who protects the limits and draws out the possibilities. She is able to consider the potential of her subject and nurture it toward maturity. The loving lord leads the created order into the way it is meant to be.

Like my daughter Simone, we have all wondered about the purpose of life. Our *raison d'etre*—our reason for being—becomes clear: we are to image God by cultivating his world as the lords who seek to bring out the potential of the creation. While distorted domination seeks to exploit something for the sake of gain, loving lordship seeks to bring out the fullness of something for the common good and for the benefit of the thing itself.

At dusk on the sixth day, God called His creation *very good*; it is perfect. So what is a perfect creation? It's a place in which all things are made according to their kind (with limits and possibilities), in right relationship with everything else made according to their kind, all under the lordship of the image-bearing humans (made according to their kind). These loving lords would not just preserve the very good kingdom; instead, they were to lead the garden from its nascent state into maturity.

This is not altogether different than a parent staring into the newly opened eyes of an infant. I looked at both of my children—even my son Gavin—born with his nose bigger than his head, and I breathed a sigh. "He is very good," I thought. The stunning thing about that moment was not only looking at this eagerly expected boy, but also understanding the possibilities of his future and knowing that he was given to me. I was the loving lord. I was a missionary tasked with bringing out his full potential and to help him understand his human limits. Maybe this is a good way to imagine the man and the woman walking in the garden.

God gave them the garden. The man and woman named and nurtured. They pruned and drew out its potential. God granted Adam and Eve perfect freedom. Their relationships (with one another, with the earth, with their work, and with God) were exactly right. The Creator King made them, and they were functioning according to their kind. Unlike today, in Eden, things were the way they were supposed to be. For the one time in all of human history the *is* was the *ought*—everything was the way it was supposed to be. Nevertheless, even this freedom held limitations.

THE GOODNESS OF LIMITATIONS

I like to ask my students this: If you could have any super-power, what would it be?[2] We go around the room. Flight always makes the top of the list. The more mischievous choose invisibility. I also hear teleportation, photographic memory, super-strength, and one joker even mentioned punctuality (if only!). After each of these I would look around the class and exclaim, "Oh, yes, that's a great one!" or "That would certainly make life better." As I belabor the point the class gets worked up into how much better life would be with these superpowers. If we could only be superhuman we might live flourishing lives.

Then I look at them and say: that's a damned (literally) lie. Remember, since God made all things according to their kind, all things, by God's law, have limits. God did not mean for humans to teleport or time travel. A desire for super-human power existed in the garden as well. God gives the man and the woman everything, but with one limitation. We read that "the LORD God commanded the man, 'You are free to eat from any tree in the garden; but you must not eat from the tree of the knowledge of good and evil, for when you eat from it you will certainly die'" (Genesis 2:16-17). Eat the cherries, the peas, and the juicy mangoes. Dig in the ground and eat the carrots and beets. Suck the juice from inside the pineapples and coco-nuts. Please, by all means, help yourself to the fruit of the Tree of Life. Freedom. But do not eat from the Tree of the Knowledge of Good and Evil. Boundary.

Scholars wrestle with this, as do I. The nature of the tree is mysterious. Likewise, it is a mystery why God placed it in the garden. However, there is some clarity as to why eating of the tree is off limits. Most of us know the story all too well. The crafty serpent manipulated the lover-lords of the garden into eating the fruit with a truth and a lie. Having heard the woman report of the impending consequence of death, he tells her, "You will not surely die." The serpent lied. Curiously, the serpent also leveraged the truth for the sake of his own Kingdom-killing mission. After his death-lie he proceeds to tell the man and the woman, "For God knows that when you eat from it your eyes will be opened, and you will be like God, knowing good and evil" (Genesis 3:5). The craftiness of the serpent rests in his ability to leverage the truth for his ends. They heard the truth and the lies. They knew the consequence. Nevertheless, they ate. As the triune God considers the sin of the man and the woman He says, "The man has now become like one of us, knowing good and evil" (Genesis 3:22). The serpent knew the effect of the fruit. The man and woman would know both good and evil and become like God.

Some religious traditions pit the gods against the humans. The gods became jealous of the humans and lusted for power over them. When I first learned this story, I read it this way. The Godhead desired man and woman not to see good and evil because of some sort of territorialism. This is precisely the wrong reading of this account. Remember, the humans were made according to their kind as image bearers of God. The image bearing nature doesn't mean that the man and woman were God, but rather they reflected Him. There remains a difference—a boundary and limitation. It was not only their possibilities, but also their limitations that made Eve and Adam human. Just like my students in the classroom, the first man and woman desired to transcend their creational boundaries. They wanted to be more than human. Their desire was to be superhumans—not just image bearers, but gods themselves.

Their actions had cosmic consequences. Everything fell apart. As we read through the effects of their choice, things become more and more devastating. A downward spiral emerges and we can see exactly what God meant by death. The moment their eyes were fully opened they saw differently. The story tells us they realized their nakedness. For the first time the woman and man were ashamed of their nakedness. To exist, before sin, was to be *open*. They maintained a posture of transparency in all aspects of their lives—toward one another, toward the created world, and toward God. But suddenly, eyes wide open, shame came into God's good creation. They fashioned the first clothing from fig leaves and covered themselves. And as the loving God—who had given them the entire world—came looking for them, in their shame, they hid from Him as well.

The first effect of sin is shame, the second is blame. When asked about eating the fruit, the man pulled a double blame move. Adam responded to his Creator by first blaming his wife. "The woman...she gave me some fruit from the tree, and I ate" (Genesis 3:12, NIV). The man knew the weight of his actions. The blame game is a long legacy that we know quite well. The shifting of responsibility from ourselves to someone else is a "natural" human response. He does not just attempt to sidestep responsibility through the woman, he actually says, "The woman *you* put here with me" (Genesis 3:12, NIV).[3] Adam looks at the gift giver and blames Eve, the greatest of His gifts. And if that is not enough, he tries to blame God. It is as if he is saying, "It's her fault Lord, but ultimately the blame is yours for putting her here with me."

Ultimately, we should always consider relational rifts as consequences of the fall into sin. Man is no longer in right relationship with woman, God, or even himself. But as mentioned before, there are other relationships as well. All of the creation is now, in the words of C.S. Lewis, "bent." The earth, once yielding its produce with ease and in abundance, becomes hard to work. Tilling becomes tedious. Bearing children, meant to be glorious and filled with joy, would now happen through pain. In the end, we see the human lords cast from the garden. Relationships with God, self, other, and creation have been torn asunder and the citizens of the Garden Kingdom have been displaced. In Milton's famous words, it was paradise lost.

But even in the midst of the curse there is hope.

Before God pronounces the effects of the disobedience He turns to the deceiver:

> The LORD God said to the serpent,
> "Because you have done this,
> cursed are you above all livestock
> and above all beasts of the field;
> on your belly you shall go,
> and dust you shall eat
> all the days of your life.
> I will put enmity between you and the woman,
> and between your offspring and her offspring;
> he shall bruise your head,
> and you shall bruise his heel." (Genesis 3:14-15)

The serpent is implicated for his cosmic role of deception. Even with the choice of the humans, he is guilty and his death sentence has been issued. The pronouncement of judgment was directed at the serpent, but it was *for* the man and the woman. In the midst of their shame and blame, while they are hiding from God and trembling in His sight, God is giving them the first message of hope in their newly distorted world. Even before He passes down their sentence, the Lord of the Kingdom makes it clear that this is not the way the story ends. This is called the protogospel—the first gospel. We do not first receive the gospel from John or even Isaiah. Gospel love and redemption is nestled right here in the third chapter of Genesis. After years of struggle there will be one who delivers the finishing blow to the crafty deceiver. And this will be Eve's offspring. Many translations render it "the Seed of the Woman."

The pronouncement was at the serpent and for the humans. However, as we consider storied leadership, we must recall that the story is being told and retold within the Israelite community. We can imagine this, can't we? Whether you believe this was written by Moses for the people of Israel during their wandering (and wondering), or if you are convinced it was written for the people in exile, the song remains the same. In the midst of struggle and uncertainty, when a people are crying out for answers to the problems with their world, as they have lost hope in the God of the universe, and when they are desiring to return to slavery or give up in a foreign land: remember the Seed of the Woman! The struggling community holds eager expectation for the Seed of the Woman. Who will restore the good, according to its kind, perfect reality that was created and set in motion in the beginning of all time? The story of the Old Testament, which often seems so foreign, is the story of this first promise, the initial covenant: the Seed of the Woman.

THE SEED OF THE WOMAN

We now know more than the Israelites. Having more of the story in hand, we now understand that the Seed of the Woman has come—not as a political revolutionary or a sword-bearing leader. Instead, the Seed of the Woman came as a babe in humble circumstances. The Seed of the Woman came as a carpenter's son who would learn and grow and build chairs alongside Joseph. He begins his ministry by telling people, here I am: the Seed of the Woman. In His first public address, we find Jesus taking the scroll of the prophet Isaiah, the old preacher of the seed of hope:

"The Spirit of the Lord is on me,
because he has anointed me
to proclaim good news to the poor.
He has sent me to proclaim freedom for the
prisoners
 and recovery of sight for the blind,
to set the oppressed free,
to proclaim the year of the Lord's favor."
(Luke 4:18-19)

The carpenter's apprentice looks up at those in the synagogue and says, "Today this scripture has been fulfilled in your hearing" (Luke 4:21). To put it another way, "Remember that story of the Seed of the Woman, the story that has brought you hope for all these years? I am the Seed. Hope is here."

What is so profound is that when Jesus reads this He is not just talking about metaphorical sight or "spiritual" freedom. The Word of God is talking about the real deal. The poor will actually receive good news, He will actually give the blind sight, and prisoners will truly be released. This is what is meant by the Lord's favor. If you don't buy this, think about what happens when John the Baptist's disciples come and ask Jesus if He is the One they have been waiting for—if He is the Seed of the Woman. Jesus says:

> Go and tell John what you hear and see: the blind receive their sight and the lame walk, lepers are cleansed and the deaf hear, and the dead are raised up, and the poor have good news preached to them. And blessed is the one who is not offended by me. (Matthew 11:4-6)

Christ tells them that He is the one the prophets spoke of. He is the Seed of the Woman.

This is the climax of the story. God made the cosmos perfect. Humans chose disobedience. All of creation was subjected to distortion. The Seed of the Woman comes as Immanuel, God with us, to restore the entirety of the creation. God does not break into the world in the flesh, to minister, heal, die a death on the cross, and rise again just to redeem human souls, but to make all bent things straight. He comes to heal the creation that "waits in eager expectation" (Romans 8:19). If you are still unsure of this grand picture of perfection distorted and restored, consider the words of the apostle Paul as he summarizes nearly the entire narrative of the scriptures:

The Son is the image of the invisible God, the first-born over all creation. For in him all things were created: things in heaven and on earth, visible and invisible, whether thrones or powers or rulers or authorities; all things have been created through him and for him. He is before all things, and in him all things hold together. And he is the head of the body, the church; he is the beginning and the first-born from among the dead, so that in everything he might have the supremacy. For God was pleased to have all his fullness dwell in him, and through him to reconcile to himself all things, whether things on earth or things in heaven, by making peace through his blood, shed on the cross. (Colossians 1:15-20)

This is the truth of the Gospel of grace: Jesus made *all* things, he sustains *all* things, and He is reconciling *all* things by his blood, shed on the cross. If we believe that the partial gospel story that Jesus died for human sin so we could go to heaven is good news, then this message is really good news. All blurriness will be focused. All bentness will be straightened. All things we create will become as they ought to be. All wounds will be healed by the blood of the Lamb—or we could say, by the piercing of the heel of the Seed of the Woman!

When Paul writes of Jesus making peace he is talking about shalom reality. This is no hippy-dippy, tie-dyed, "peace, man" proclamation. This is the peace that is manifested when Jesus returns things to being "according to their kind" and sets them in right relationship with everything else "according to their kind." The blood of the lamb for the peace of the nations is a correction of all that has gone wrong and the utter perfection of things already considered good!

This is the story. The story we live in and lead out of. But if we read well and observe the current state of the world, it looks like this shalom Kingdom is *not* a reality. As we consider our friends, our colleagues, and ourselves we know that parents still get divorced, little babies are still born with diseases, the work of studying for a test is still difficult, children are still emotionally and physically abused, we still suffer heartbreak, friends still cut themselves to deal with pain, our cars still break down, mosquitoes still bite, multi-national corporations still pollute, we are still afraid for others to know who we really are, kids still go to bed hungry, tsunamis and tornados still wipe out entire communities, eating disorders still ravage our minds and bodies, people are still captured in slavery, and we still—no matter how hard we try or how long we pray—are captured by our deep and damaging habitual sins.

On our worst days these present realities whisper to us, "It can't be true. The story is a lie." On our best day we remain in hope. The Bible, our great narrative about reality, does not just tell the story of the past and the present. It is also teleological—it has a goal toward which it is directed.

Like the first man and woman, like the Israelites exiled to Babylon, like the early persecuted church, we must remember that the ultimate story of the culmination of our hope is about the future. Even now we look forward to the second coming of the Seed of the Woman as told to us by the John in the book of Revelation:

Then I saw a new heaven and a new earth, for the first heaven and the first earth had passed away, and the sea was no more. And I saw the holy city, new Jerusalem, coming down out of heaven from God, prepared as a bride adorned for her husband. And I heard a loud voice from the throne saying, "Behold, the dwelling place of God is with man. He will dwell with them, and they will be his people, and God himself will be with them as their God. He will wipe away every tear from their eyes, and death shall be no more, neither shall there be mourning, nor crying, nor pain anymore, for the former things have passed away." And he who was seated on the throne said, "Behold, I am making all things new." Also he said, "Write this down, for these words are trustworthy and true." (Revelation 21:1-5)

And he continues in the final chapter of the entire narrative:

Then the angel showed me the river of the water of life, bright as crystal, flowing from the throne of God and of the Lamb through the middle of the street of the city; also, on either side of the river, the tree of life with its twelve kinds of fruit, yielding its fruit each month. The leaves of the tree were for the healing of the nations. No longer will there be anything accursed, but the throne of God and of the Lamb will be in it, and his servants will worship him. They will see his face, and his name will be on their foreheads. And night will be no more. They will need no light of lamp or sun, for the Lord God will be their light, and they will reign forever and ever. (Revelation 22:1-5)

I read this every semester to students in large lecture halls and small discussion rooms. I read it as often as I can. I read it for them, but more so, I read it for me. With all of the deep aches of this present reality, the story continues to turn our eyes toward the Seed of the Woman. Jesus, the Lamb-King, is coming again to make everything new—the trees and the bees, our bodies, the work of our hands, and our relationships. And don't miss this; in this New Heaven and New Earth, fully developed to its potential, we find the return of one of the trees—The Tree of Life.

The narrative is eternal. It's a forever story.

FOR DISCUSSION OR REFLECTION:

1. Is this telling of the story of the gospel different than the one you are accustomed to? How so?

2. What stood out to you about the story of the scriptures? How might it change your view of reality?

3. Can you identify significant ways that this narrative might affect your perspective on leadership?

CHAPTER 3
Cultivate and Restore

Leadership is shaped by stories about reality. These narratives shape and influence certain conceptions of what leadership is, how to lead, and what to lead toward. If this is true, then a more accurate story about reality will offer a more authentic paradigm for leadership. Distorted views of reality will always incite distortions in leadership.

We often merge the western story—which idealizes progress, individualism, and consumerism—with a truncated gospel. Many churches reduce the gospel to an insurance plan to escape the fiery pits of hell and, perhaps, a set of moral imperatives to guide us as we await eternal bliss. The scriptures are sometimes referred to as an "instruction manual," outlining ways to dwell in this world as we wait for the next. The confluence of an American worldview and a truncated gospel creates a church that often consists of consumers here and now, waiting for a better place beyond.

A consideration of the long story of God, His people, their place, and their calling throughout the scriptures disavows both of these perspectives and certainly the synchronism of the western story and a truncated gospel. An explicit engagement with the narrative-whole is crucial to investigate a Kingdom perspective on leadership.

KINGDOM CALLINGS

All stories have a *telos*—that is, a goal toward which they are directed. We can think of some of the most beloved adventure stories: *The Lord of the Rings*, *Harry Potter*, *Star Wars*, or The *Odyssey*. The story drives the plot through space and time. Whether drawn into the adventure by fate, position, or birthright, the characters are often gripped by an epic purpose: destroy the ring, defeat the nefarious lord, overcome the evil empire, or, simply (but not so easily) make it home.

Storied leadership requires an understanding of the purposes of the characters—what we are to do. So, who are we in the narrative of the scriptures? Humans are in the midst of the story as image bearers of the Creator King and heirs to His Kingdom. We are made like God. As daughters and sons, we not only inherit the Kingdom itself, but the *Missio Dei*: the mission of God.

The inheritance of the Kingdom includes the call of the Kingdom. What exactly is this call? Remember the question of my daughter Simone, "What is it all about anyway?" For the remainder of this chapter, and ultimately for the rest of the book, we will consider the call of God to us as heirs of His Kingdom.

Often times the evangelical church has reduced the *Missio Dei* to what is often called the Great Commission. For years, I believed this as well. Once called into relationship with Jesus, our calling is to save other souls and wait for the magnificent returning of our Lord. The Great Commission, found in the Gospel of Matthew reads:

> Then Jesus came to them and said, "All authority in heaven and on earth has been given to me. Therefore go and make disciples of all nations, baptizing them in the name of the Father and of the Son and of the Holy Spirit, and teaching them to obey everything I have commanded you. And surely I am with you always, to the very end of the age."
> (Matthew 28:18-20, NIV)

Many believe that according to this passage we are to lead people into a saving knowledge of, and relationship with, the triune God through the redemptive work of Jesus Christ for the sake of an eternal destiny. Are we to do this? Absolutely. However, this Great Commission is often truncated to *only* that. If we read the passage with wide eyes and open minds we see something more than just the eternal salvation of individuals.

This Great Commission is actually a threefold command. The first two imperatives are often the most evident. First, we are told to make disciples of everyone, regardless of race, class, or location. The reader is also instructed that those drawn into a relationship of the Master Discipler are then to be baptized. What does this mean? Once someone is led into relationship of Christ, they are baptized into the community of believers. In my tradition we consider baptism the "sign and seal of the covenant family."

However, there is a third piece of the command that is too often neglected. As friends become followers of Jesus, welcomed into the community of grace, we are then to teach them everything Jesus has commanded us. That's a tall order. The curriculum of the disciple, the everything that Jesus commanded, is not just the words of Christ exhibited in the gospels. It is also the story of the people of Israel, the words of the prophets and psalmists, the letters of the New Testament, and even the vision of John of the New Heavens and New Earth.

What's the everything? It's the story. Teach them the unfolding drama of the scriptures, from beginning to end. The amazing thing about teaching the narrative of the Bible is that we are not only instructing our children, our friends, and our coworkers *what to do*, but we are also teaching them *who they are*—who they are called to *be*. The Kingdom gospel is not only about doing, but it is always about being. The fascinating thing is that our doing always emerges from our being. So it is with our leadership. Leading does not emerge only from what the leader is to do, but who the leader is.

CALLED TO BE CULTIVATORS AND RESTORERS
When I was ten years old I began a bizarre hobby that would haunt me socially for years. Almost perfectly timed with the onset of puberty, my parents signed me up for a dog-showing club. While other kids were perfecting their fastballs or learning to play Led Zeppelin tunes on a six string, I was prancing around in a circle with a canine. My coolness was overwhelming. While that should be embarrassing enough, the most humiliating part was that I didn't have a dog. My sister was handling Sam, our old beagle, but I was a dogless dog shower. I still went to the club, but I would arrive and pick up a loaner. She was nice

enough, and cute, but she certainly was not mine. After months, I finally got the chance to pick out my own dog. I surveyed a group of puppies. "That one," I said. "That one is *good*." Bandit was a good dog. On the ride home my dad said to me, "Son, now it's your job to make that pup into a champion." A champion? She would not sit, stay, or heel. For that matter she didn't even know her name. After years of training she became an amazing show dog. She became so attuned to the work of the ring that she would strut her stuff with elegance. Bandit would turn on a dime and respond to the slightest movement of the leash. My dog was awarded Best in Breed on several occasions. Thinking back to that first moment when I saw her in the pen, I could see that she was a good dog. Yet, I had to imagine what she could become. My parents gave me a dog—she was mine. With the gift of the dog, all packed with potential, they also gave me a task. Take the shivering, shy puppy and make her great. Make her what she ought to be.

Whether it is a dog to be trained, a lump of moist clay to be molded, a business plan to be written, or a fellowship program to be developed, I think that we can all recall a time when we realized that something was packed with potential, ready to be shaped into something different, something more. In the grand story of the Bible there was a similar moment. After the Creator had made the land, sea, and sky—when it was filled with plants and teaming with creatures—He made the humans. Standing before the good and wild place God gave the first commandment. He gave a Kingdom calling.

Cultivate

A vision of who we are in the Kingdom is the beginning of our leadership. As we read the scriptures we come to find the setting of the story. We also discover where the narrative is going. The epic Christian tale is always one moving from the garden Kingdom of Genesis, through the Kingdom inaugurated by Jesus, and toward a City Garden as seen in Revelation. And within the story of the Kingdom we must understand our role as characters in the tale.

In the story of Creation, we have the first command to the humans. In the first chapter we read it this way: "And God blessed them, saying, 'Be fruitful and multiply and fill the waters in the seas, and let birds multiply on the earth'" (Genesis 1:22). In chapter two we read: "The LORD God took the man and put him in the garden of Eden to work it and keep it" (Genesis 2:15). Being human is embodying the image of God in the creation. The primary aspect of this imaging God is to create! It is one of the first things told about God in the story of the scriptures. He is a creator. If we are to image God, we too are to make things. The image bearer is to fill the earth. The filling is not a thoughtless act, but it is to care for the creation.

There are several translations of the phrase "to work it and take care of it," as rendered by the New International Version and the English Standard Version. The Revised Standard Version translates the Hebrew term as to "till it and keep it." These translations evidently bring out the initial command to the people of the garden. God gives them the entire place, with all of its potential, and commands them to develop it and to care for it.

While these iterations of the command are accurate,

they are steeped in the connotation of a "garden." Perhaps the New American Standard Bible is more helpful. There the translators choose the word "cultivate." Cultivation is an agrarian term, but it holds a much broader connotation. Cultivation comes from the Latin *colere*—literally to till or to guard. At the very foundation of being human, made in the image of God, is to till the creation and to guard it.

At the root of cultivation we see the very familiar word *cult*. Often we think of cults as offshoots of legitimate religious communities or even radical fringe groups. The etymology of cult—from the Latin *cultus*—maintains the notion of care and labor. *Cultus* also means culture. That is, the fruit of our careful labor. What is fascinating is that *cultus* also means worship. The first command of cultivation encapsulates what it means to be human in the good Kingdom of God: to care for the world, but also to work *on* the world. To cultivate is to worship. Making culture out of the world in which we live is an act of suitable worship unto God himself. As we bear the image of God as creators, we worship Him through this image-bearing work. This changes everything. Discipleship is not only learning to read the scriptures, pray, and fast. It also includes learning to be cultivators.

Care-filled creation is found throughout the narrative of the scriptures. We find it in the first humans when Adam names the creatures. This is not just a mere naming, but a taxonomy. Adam sees, studies, and categorizes every living thing. The chapter of the Bible best known for the devastating murder of Abel by his brother Cain also tells us of Tubal-Cain, who forged all kinds of tools from iron, and Jubal, the father of all who made beautiful music on pipes and stringed instruments. All of them were cultivators.

Jethro helped Moses to shape a governing system that would serve the people. Miriam wrote music. Huram was filled with wisdom, knowledge, and understanding. He crafted pillars and pomegranates of bronze for the temple. Peter, James, and John made intricate fishing nets. All of them were cultivators. Throughout the scriptures we find artists, artisans, architects, governors, and grandparents. All of them tilled the creation and brought out the potential that lies within it.

This command to cultivate is critical to the work of leadership in God's world. We are called to lead the nascent creation from potentiality into actuality. To shape the world and develop it, to till it and guard it, is the imperative. The leader who designs a neighborhood outreach program for other students is making culture. The teacher who crafts curricula for the classroom and the chemist who develops lifesaving drugs are making culture. The musician who picks up a guitar and works out a riff is making culture. Each of these acts of cultivation. When done well, they are "influencing purposeful positive changes." We will later exhibit how these are done in fullness with others. Making culture is faithfulness to our image, and in this we worship the creator God. This is what we mean by storied leadership.

Guard and till. Preserve and cultivate. These poignant commands are for all of us. They are a summons to leadership of the creation in the Kingdom. As image bearers, we are all leaders. Part of the call is to create culture and make stuff—from the papers written for classes to the lines of software code hammered out late into the night.

Christians who truly have a Kingdom vision of reality—who pray, "Your Kingdom come, Your will be done, on earth as it is in heaven"—need to consider how to go about creating culture and leading others toward their potential. They have a different way of being in all areas of their lives. Our intent is not to write an instruction manual or a list of techniques. Rather, we want to offer ways of being in the world as image bearers of the one true God who are called to cultivate His beautiful world because we are convinced that who we are as heirs to the Kingdom affects what we do in the Kingdom.

Restore

We know that the original call—to subdue and fill the earth and to be guardians and cultivators of the creation—took a fatal turn. Thinking of ourselves as leaders only in a world of possibility falls short if we neglect the cosmic effects of sin. All has been distorted. With the loss of the perfect garden Kingdom, the calling is expanded. Prior to the Fall, people were called to be cultivators. No longer do we reside in the infant earth of Eden. Leading in the world currently is no longer only taking a perfectly good (yet immature) place and making full with culture. Our role as image bearers is also the work of reconciliation. In the beginning, God made stuff and said, "Now, you be like Me and make stuff." After the Fall, Christ comes into the world and says, "Through My ministry, life, death, and resurrection, I am making all things new. I have come to reconcile all things." God's message remains. "Now, be like Me, be ambassadors of reconciliation."

My friend Patrick is an amazing luthier. A luthier is a craftsperson trained in the art of making fretted stringed instruments. After months of intensive training he opened a little storefront in Canton, Ohio. He named it New Vintage Music. The name encapsulates the mission of his work. Patrick takes slabs of unfinished wood and shapes them into beautiful electric guitars. His work is phenomenal. This is a perfect example of a creator taking raw materials in the world and making them into something brand new—drawing out the potential.

Patrick realizes that creation is not the only work at hand in the guitar world. Another passion of his is in restoration. He is a master of taking a guitar that has been ruined by water damage, broken by a fall, or generally mishandled for years and renewing it. In his work of restoration, Patrick is able to see the instrument according to what it was meant to be and what it once was. Then he goes to work, fixing the problems that have deeply distorted the once beautiful instrument. The results are breathtaking. It is frequently more impressive than the making of a new instrument. While the restorative process is often more difficult than a new creation, it is worth every stroke of the file.

There is yet another area of the guitar world that Patrick deals in—and perhaps it occupies the majority of his time. It is called doing a "set up." A set up is neither the creation of something new, nor a massive restoration, but rather it is performing a deep tuning. Set ups always involves a careful cleaning and new strings. Sometimes frets are filed, abolishing buzzing during play. While a set up doesn't result in the evidently transformative results of a new build or restoration, it is nevertheless crucial to maintaining the goodness of the guitar.

Patrick's work is a clear picture of the call to the Kingdom-minded Christians. We are certainly called to bring out the potential through new creations, but often we are called to fix things. All around us are aspects of God's good creation that have been fouled. This hard work of restoring something with obvious defects can lead to grand and often awe-inspiring effects. When Patrick posts before and after shots of a tedious restoration they draw many "oohs and ahs." More often than not, our work of Kingdom leadership is not the craft of a grand creation or even of significant restoration. We usually find ourselves doing "set ups" in the world. This could include tweaking a human resources process we have adopted or configuring ways for our churches' small groups to utilize new media more fruitfully. More often than not, our work is the fine tuning of things already in place.

Set ups are not always exciting or sexy. They seldom result in noticeable change or praise from our colleagues. These works are just as important as the others. Fine tuning the world around us is necessary. Seeing the way in which things have gone slightly "out of tune" and redirecting them toward the way they ought to be is some of the most important work of our hands. Sometimes the Kingdom leader is called lead their community to cultivate the good creation toward being filled with new, beautiful, and helpful things. At other times it is taking the systems, institutions, people, and practices that surround us and redirecting them toward major restoration.

Frequently, as leaders, our goal is that of fine tuning and making the world more like the Kingdom as God intended it to be.

HEARING, SEEING, IMAGINING, ACTING

While in no way formulaic, the work of cultivators and restorers often progresses through four stages. *Hearing* the call is the first step. As we have already argued, the narrative of the scriptures calls us to be tellers and doers of the good news, that Jesus died to reconcile all things and ultimately to make all of the earth new. The obedient life is one that encapsulates the call to evangelism and more. We are also commanded to cultivate and care for the world. Christians who understand the grand narrative can come to realize this commission.

The second step is *seeing* the created order as it presently is. One author who has captured the hearts and minds of many of my friends and colleagues is the poet-farmer Wendell Berry. Berry is prolific. He is a writer of fiction, non-fiction, and poetry. His fiction revolves around the life of Port William, an elaborate world parallel to Berry's own town of Port Royal, Kentucky. The chronicles of Port William begin in 1888, in a world of steam boats and horse-drawn buggies, and finds its culmination in 2001 in the context of Gameboys and creeping suburbs.

While my tech-loving, urban-dwelling friends do not aspire to all of the farmer-poet's particularities regarding life, they are drawn to many of his fundamental commitments. Perhaps the most captivating is Berry's topophilia—his love of place—which finds its genesis in one seeing clearly. He writes, "One loves the place because present appearances recommend it, and because they suggest possibilities irresistibly imaginable."[1] We do not truly love anything because of what it might grant us—this instead is lust or perhaps desire. We love something because the thing itself "recommends" loving it. This is true for Patrick when he sees a guitar in disrepair and for me when I see students who are hungry to explore ideas. I imagine it is true for you in your corner of the Kingdom. The present image of God's world causes us to love it as it is—in all of its brokenness.

This present image beckons us to have a vision of a future; how things might be. Berry continues, "One's head, like a lover's, grows full of visions. One walks over the premises, saying, 'If this were mine, I'd make a permanent pasture here; here is where I'd plant an orchard; here is where I'd dig a pond.' These visions are the usual stuff of unfulfilled love and induce wakefulness at night."[2] The farmer imagines a possible future for the place. *Imagining* the future is the third step. Like the kid who sees a large oak tree and imagines an elaborate fort with spires, ladders, and a fireman's pole, there is something intrinsically human about seeing potential. The pastor imagines the community that has worked through deeply rooted conflicts. The credit union president considers how a financial institution could work for the common good of a local community. The storied leader imagines how things could be different in their fellowship group or on the little league field. They imagine what a more robust multi-cultural community could look like. They imagine a local government that has real and lasting representation of the citizens of the town. They imagine how a team could not only win games, but affect change in the community.

Finally, we are moved to *act*. The garden Kingdom—with all of its potential—recommends its development. Hearing the command, seeing the way things are, and imagining the way they might be is all neutered by passivity.

*The leader does not only see that things are
distorted and imagine a better reality,
but they must also work for restoration.*

Of course, action looks differently depending on the field
in which you work. For many, this is the hardest part of
the process. It is often easy to see problems and exciting
to imagine the future. Action requires commitment and
the (often) long, hard work of moving toward the vision.
Hearing the call. *Seeing* the world. *Imagining* the future
potentialities. *Acting* toward fullness. Berry encapsulates
the great commandment in its fullness. Yet, the poet-
farmer is not only concerned with the virgin soil ripe for
new cultivation. More often than not he considers the old
broken down farm, injured and worn by misuse and abuse.
He sees the land distorted by the laziness, selfishness,
arrogance, and ignorance of previous owners. Berry is not
only captured by the vision to create something wholly
new, but is also inspired to heal that which is broken. This
is not unlike the way that Paul explains the post-fall state
of God's world:

> For the creation was subjected to futility, not will-
> ingly, but because of him who subjected it, in hope
> that the creation itself will be set free from its bond-
> age to corruption and obtain the freedom of the
> glory of the children of God. For we know that the
> whole creation has been groaning together in the
> pains of childbirth until now. (Romans 8:20-22)

The creation groans for redemption; it calls out for the
crucified King to reconcile it toward the way it ought to

be. We are the ambassadors of that very reconciliation. When Paul speaks of the creation, he is not just speaking of the "earth." Rather, he is concerned with all parts of the creation—including the cultural landscape. The groaning occurs in businesses, schools, families, and governmental structures. All of these are aspects of the creation developed into culture. In each there are glimpses of goodness, but also signs of misdirection. Or as Simone Weil describes, it is a world that has encountered both gravity and grace.[3]

When my son Gavin was a newborn, I knew he was very good. He couldn't do a thing except eat, cry, and poop. Yet, I saw goodness not only in the fact that he had come into the world, but also because he was mine. Like all children (and adults), he is not always the way he ought to be. While made by the good grace of God, he is soiled by the Fall as well. As a parent, my task is to help bring out the good things that await cultivation. My task is also to try, by the grace of God, to reshape the things that are not quite right. Day to day, the loving care that I give is not encapsulated by shaping "new" aspects of my son or even righting some terrible wrong. Rather, it is often the work of daily tuning.

As we recall the story of the scriptures, we must remember that it is not an abstraction set apart from our ever-present reality. Rather, it is a story written for us, to us, and, ultimately, about us. Kingdom leaders are those who deny a truncated gospel and realize that the words of the Lord's Prayer implicate us: "Your Kingdom come, Your will be done, on earth as it is in Heaven." Faithfulness is hearing the call, seeing the world in its potential and brokenness, imagining the possibilities, and endeavoring toward them. Knowing the human role as characters

FOR DISCUSSION OR REFLECTION:

1. What are ways that you already see yourself as a cultivator and restorer?

2. Can you identify times when you have done the work of fine-tuning? What did the work involve? How are these tasks important? Did the work seem to go unnoticed? How did this feel?

3. Consider a current area or situation in which you have influence. Now reflect on or talk about the ways that seeing the current state of things and imagining how things ought to be. How do these impact your vision for cultivating in that area?

CHAPTER 4
Kingdom Collaboration

Finding words that accurately describe leadership is difficult. It is a topic of deep complexity and countless definitions. Over the years I have found very little solace in capturing the fullness of what I want to communicate when it comes to a robust description of leadership. Then a number of years ago, my friend and colleague Don Opitz described Christian leadership as "Kingdom collaboration."[1] This conception has influenced my thinking and teaching ever since.

Earlier, we referenced one of my favorite Bible passages—a fulfillment of an Old Testament story. In the book of Luke we find that John the Baptist is imprisoned and, I'm assuming, fighting a bit of discouragement, frustration, and doubt. He has had quite the journey, experiencing some incredible things as he prepared the way for the coming Messiah. Perhaps John is starting to have second thoughts about Jesus. We read, "...and John, calling two of his disciples to him, sent them to the Lord, saying, 'Are you the one who is to come, or shall we look for another?'" (Luke 7:19). Let's take a step back for a moment:

In those days Jesus came from Nazareth of Gal-
ilee and was baptized by John in the Jordan. And
when He came up out of the water, immediately He
saw the heavens being torn open and the Spirit de-
scending on Him like a dove. And a voice came from
heaven, 'You are My beloved Son; with You I am well
pleased.' (Mark 1:9-11)

Yes, that's right. John baptized Jesus and he witnesses this
firsthand. John sees the heavens open and observes Jesus
being blessed by His father—right there, with his own
eyes. But, now we find him doubting. His perspective has
been clouded and skewed. John the Baptist had allowed
his current circumstances to take over his thinking.

Jesus reminds them of the Seed of the Woman, "And He
answered them, 'Go and tell John what you have seen and
heard: the blind receive their sight, the lame walk, lepers
are cleansed, and the deaf hear, the dead are raised up, the
poor have good news preached to them'" (Luke 7:22). Jesus
doesn't even directly answer the question. He instead replies
with a call to recognize the fulfillment of prophecies.

Jesus' response does not serve only John. He obviously
knew of John's discouraging predicament. I like to think
that part of the message that Jesus was sending back to
John included something like, "Hey, snap out of it. This
thing is way bigger than you." Did Jesus care about John
and the situation he was in? Of course, he also understood the context of the Kingdom and that something even
greater was at work. John needed a refocusing moment, a
paradigm shift. What can we pick up on here? It is all about
the Kingdom—which is all of God's creation as it ought
to be. It's always about the Kingdom. Our perspective and

our leadership needs to be embedded in this Kingdom perspective. As one theologian wrote, "Nothing matters but the Kingdom, but because of the Kingdom, everything matters."[2]

Our leadership begins with a Kingdom perspective, it points toward a Kingdom vision, and it should always end with a Kingdom purpose. It is impossible to overdo it here. We are simply following the example of Jesus who was always talking about the Kingdom. Everything was in reference to, and constantly pointing toward, the Kingdom—"the Kingdom of God is like a seed," "the Kingdom of God is like a treasure," "the Kingdom of God is like a net," and so on. Always the Kingdom. If we can start to imagine a world that glorifies God—peace not turmoil, love not hate, mercy not selfishness, forgiveness not blame, joy not sorrow—then we will get a small glimpse of how Jesus was entirely Kingdom-crazy. This is the story that shapes our leadership. It is a story that solicits a response.

When we know something about the world we live in, we must respond. We must move. Leaders must figure out how to respond to the world they live in. We are responsible for what we know about the world. Steve Garber asks the question that every leader should consider, "Knowing what you know about the world, what are you going to do about it?"[3] The Kingdom story mandates a response from the Christian leader. When we are captured by a Kingdom vision, by a picture of what could be and should be, something ignites within us and we move. Leadership is about a movement toward a better world.

OUR DESIGN

Responding to what we know about the world should never be done alone. Leadership is never a solo affair. While parts of the process are often done alone, leadership is a process that should involve a group. Leaders and followers are always working together toward positive purposeful changes. Even Patrick, the guitar builder from earlier in the book, has been influenced, guided, and supported by a community. This is why leadership is so wonderfully captured by the concept of Kingdom collaboration.

Leadership is collaborative first and foremost because of our design. It is important to keep in mind that we are *Imago Dei*. We are created to reflect the image of God and live out our image-bearing responsibilities. God is communal in His triune nature. Genesis makes this clear: "Then God said, 'Let us make mankind in our image, in our likeness'" (Genesis 1:26, NIV). God Himself exists in community. We best reflect Him when we ourselves are living and working with others toward a better world.

Not only is it a part of our image-bearing responsibility, we also see a clear description in the scriptures of the need to operate as the body, the Apostle Paul makes this evident in I Corinthians. He writes, "For the body does not consist of one member but of many," and continues, "But as it is, God arranged the members in the body, each one of them, as He chose. If all were a single member, where would the body be? As it is, there are many parts, yet one body" (I Corinthians 12:12, 19-120). As Christian leaders, we work together as the body that Paul is describing, and we function as an integrated whole. God has wired this into our design.

C.S. Lewis addresses the concept of the body of Christ in *The Weight of Glory* by using the analogy of organs functioning together. He writes, "By members [St. Paul] meant what we should call organs, things essentially different from, and complementary to, one another, things differing not only in structure and function but also in dignity." Using the membership of a family as an example, he goes on, "If you subtract any one member, you have not simply reduced the family in number; you have inflicted an injury on its structure."[4] Our design, the structure that God Himself has put in place, is one of membership. In the perfect garden, God made it clear that we were not supposed to be alone. In the wilderness, the Israelites wandered together. Even Jesus had His twelve disciples. We are made to follow these examples and live as co-laborers.

The time of apartheid in South Africa is one of humanity's darkest moments. In the 1940s the country classified inhabitants into racial groups and mandated segregated residential areas. The word *apartheid* is literally interpreted "the state of being apart." It means disintegration. In the early 1990s, things began to change with new legislation and governmental elections—particularly with the presidential election, resulting in the victory of Nelson Mandela. A rare and powerful movement followed enacted by the Truth & Reconciliation Commission (TRC). Attempting to carry out restorative-justice, the TRC brought together victims and perpetrators in striving for forgiveness, reconciliation, and amnesty.

One of the leading voices of the TRC was Archbishop Desmond Tutu. A recipient of the Nobel Peace Prize in 1984, Tutu found himself called out of retirement to lead what resulted in one of the most powerful acts of justice the modern world has experienced. Tutu described this movement in his book *No Future without Forgiveness*. It is a powerful depiction of grace, forgiveness, and reintegration. One of the primary foci of the book is the idea of *Umbuntu*. A concept without a simple translation, Umbuntu is the idea that our individual identities are wrapped up with those that we live among. One particular definition translated by Liberian peace activist Leymah Gbowee is: "I am what I am because of who we all are."[5] Tutu reiterates in his words:

> One of the sayings in our country is Ubuntu—the essence of being human. Ubuntu speaks particularly about the fact that you can't exist as a human being in isolation. It speaks about our interconnectedness. You can't be human all by yourself, and when you have this quality—Ubuntu—you are known for your generosity. We think of ourselves far too frequently as just individuals, separated from one another, whereas you are connected and what you do affects the whole World. When you do well, it spreads out; it is for the whole of humanity.[6]

This is our design. I can't be me—and you can't be you—in isolation.

We each fulfill our image-bearing responsibilities by participating in the world together.

We need each other. It is in our wiring. Dr. Henry Cloud uses the following analogy that drives this point home:

One of my favorite studies was done years ago with monkeys, measuring the effects of relationships on cortisol levels in the brain. (Cortisol is a hormone associated with high levels of stress.) In this particular experiment, a monkey was put in a cage and exposed to a high level of psychological stress, including loud noises and flashing lights. They pretty much scared him to death. When the monkey was totally terrified, the scientists took a baseline measure of stress hormone levels in the monkey's brain as it was exposed to these stressors. Next, the researchers introduced one change into the experiment: they opened the door and put a buddy, another monkey, into the cage. That was it. They exposed the monkeys to the same loud noises and flashing lights, and then took another measure of stress hormones. The result? The level of stress hormones in the brain had dropped in half. The lone monkey was only half as good at handling stress as the pair was together. So my question for you guys... who's your monkey?![7]

This truly is the way that our Creator created us and intends for us to operate. We all need a monkey, or two, or three. Our lives will be better lived when we accept that we need community. Leaders will be exponentially better when they realize that leading is never a solo affair, but a process that can only be executed together. This is why Kingdom collaboration encapsulates the idea of Christian leadership so perfectly.

EFFECTIVE

A great team is a powerful thing. Consider the story of the 1980 U.S. Olympic Men's Hockey Team. This group of young men overcame obstacles and mind-boggling odds to win the gold medal after beating the Russian team in the semifinals. No one thought they had a chance of winning since the Russians had won the previous sixteen years of gold medals.

Much of the success of that team was attributed to the coach, Herb Brooks. In the 2004 film adaptation, *Miracle*, there is a poignant scene that depicts Brooks trying to assemble his team at a national tryout. As Brooks is observing some of the best hockey players in the country, his assistant coach walks up with the roster that Brooks has assembled and says, "You're missing some of the best players." Without missing a beat Brooks responds, "I'm not looking for the best players, Craig. I'm looking for the right ones." Herb Brooks knew what a great team could achieve. He understood the effectiveness of choosing the right people to perform collectively. It worked. With very little time together, and low expectation of winning from his counterparts, Brooks created a team that accomplished the unthinkable.

How powerful is a team of people working together? Author and leadership consultant Patrick Lencioni explains that "teamwork remains the ultimate competitive advantage, both because it is so powerful and so rare."[8] Leaders must understand their key plays and harness the potential and effectiveness of their team.

Consider the range and efficiency geese achieve when they execute the V formation. It is particularly true when migrating long distances. If there are twenty-five birds flying in this formation, each bird can experience a reduction of induced drag of up to 65%—as a result, the range of distance for the group can increase by 71%. This allows them to migrate thousands of miles due to their inherent design. Our own nature is collaborative; it is the way that God intended it. Our leadership is no different. When you participate in the process of leadership, you are contributing to something greater than yourself—something that cannot be done by just you alone. It is intended to be done together.

AND YET, MESSY

I will be one of the first to admit that working with others can often feel harder than leading alone. Leadership doesn't always feel like an Olympic hockey team or a traveling gaggle of geese. Sometimes it just feels messy.

Late one summer, Keith and I spent a weekend with a small group of friends at a cabin in the hills of northwestern Pennsylvania. We enjoyed conversations, catching up with one another, and marveled at the wonderful creation along the river. On Saturday morning we decided to take canoes out on the Allegheny River. I jumped into one with my friend Scott and we started paddling up stream. We enjoyed the landscape as we discussed life, work, and ideas. After a while, the group decided to head back down river. As Scott and I became lost in conversation we soon discovered that not only had we ended up on the opposite side of the river from the group, but we had also run into shallow water—so shallow that our canoe would not budge. Carrying our canoe to deeper waters, we realized

we were still far from where our group had stopped. Now
further downstream, we needed to paddle back upstream
against the flow.

At this point in the story, I could easily discuss the bene-
fits of working together. We needed to work as a team to get
to where we wanted, by communicating well and paddling
in tandem. That would be a perfect example of accomplishing more together. But that is not what happened.
Teamwork is often difficult and can look differently than
what we expect. Scott and I did work together to make our
way back to the group. Nearing our group, a friend from
the shore was yelling some sort of warning, but it was too
late. An avid paddler would have seen the wicked current
we were attempting to cross—we did not. We capsized and
lost all orientation to where we were.

Of the guys that were there on the shore, some laughed.
Others went into action. The canoe had started downstream so a couple of them retrieved it. Our minimal
belongings went everywhere and some of the group
retrieved those. Keith went on an immediate rescue oper-
ation for my shoes that had taken off at a high speed
down the river. When all was said and done, Scott and I
were drenched and trying to figure out where everything
was, Keith had a bloodied and broken toe, and the bag
of chips was lost forever.

The result, however, was accomplished through working together, as disordered as it was. Teamwork can be
messy business. Leadership is often messy work, but it
is good. It is work that we are designed to do together.
It will never be perfect, as we will discuss more in depth
later; but we can get close. We can actively participate

in the leadership process and move closer to the *ought* as we do so.

> *Leadership from a Christian perspective is Kingdom collaboration.*

The Christian leader accepts the responsibility to act on what he knows about the world and faithfully participates in the community of image bearers. You are responsible with what you know about whatever sphere of influence you are in. Respond to the opportunities that could make the world a little better in these areas. Together, we join in the mission of God in the world and continually work to advance His Kingdom.

FOR REFLECTION AND DISCUSSION:

1. Is there a particular vision that you have that would contribute to a better world?

2. How do you influence others to "move" with what they know about the world?

3. Henry Cloud asks, "Who is your monkey?" Who is it? Who are the people that you go to in times of need and when you need support? List them. Thank them.

4. Are there hurdles that are prohibiting you from leading more collaboratively? Identify potential solutions to overcome these.

CHAPTER 5

His Gift, Our Response

I looked up from my plate of chicken marsala and asked, "What is it that makes it so ridiculously popular?" A group of colleagues were enjoying food and conversation with a speaker from out of town. Those gathered were deep thinkers about the nature of popular artifacts including music, film, and television; so it seemed the perfect time to ask about the book that had taken over our campus. From time to time, a novel will capture the hearts and minds of our students. Recently a book grabbed their imaginations. In fact, it was not just one book, but three—the *Hunger Games* trilogy by Suzanne Collins.

The story takes place in Panem, a land ruled by a tyrant. The government had put down an attempted revolution and, as a way to remind the people of their place and the power of the government, the rulers established the annual Hunger Games. In these games, the names of two children from each of the land's districts were chosen to enter the arena for a fight to the death. The story's protagonist, Katniss Everdeen, is the quintessential scapegoat. She volunteers to take the place of her younger sister, whose name is drawn, in *The Hunger Games*. Katniss trades her own life for her sister's.

Watching this book's popularity spread like wildfire, I wondered why so many were enthralled by the tales. What was it that so drew us into the story of Katniss? Further, and perhaps more importantly, what does this narrative tell us about ourselves? Culture serves as a mirror, showing who we are and what we desire. We are drawn into stories of our times—movies, music, and visual art—because they portray something that connects with our own experiences. The narratives also show what we hope for in life.

Collins created the perfect storm for a best seller: government oppression, a young female protagonist, a love triangle, and the possibility of overcoming adversity against all odds. All of these aspects of *The Hunger Games* can connect with our feelings about the world. However, I think there is something more that subtly draws people into the narrative. There was another theme that stood out again and again as I read: indebtedness. Not only of a debt owed, but also of debts that cannot be repaid. We see this primarily through our protagonist Katniss who is offered unearned grace by Peeta—the boy who enters the games with her. In a flashback we find young Peeta giving bread to Katniss who is a half-orphaned child searching for food in the back alleyways of her district.

Years later, in the arena, Peeta risks his life again to save Katniss. In a telling line, she says, "If, in fact, Peeta did save me, I'm in his debt again. And this can't be paid back."[1] For Katniss, and for many of us, receiving a gift is an excruciating experience. She is shaken by the fact that Peeta has risked all to save her. What is more, Katniss is in her situation because she traded her own life to preserve the life of her sister. She gives everything to save the one she loves. The heroine grants the greatest gift, yet still has an inability to accept a gift in kind given over to her. Gifts are granted throughout *The Hunger Games*. The gifts that are given are not intended to create a debt; they are free of charge. In many ways we are exactly like Katniss. As leaders in God's world, we have likely sacrifices of many things—wealth, prestige, or precious time. Yet, just like Katniss, many of us loathe the idea of receiving an undeserved gift from another.

This web of gifting and indebtedness leads us to consider the ultimate Gift Giver. God gave us a gift of the creation, which requires a response. He, who gave us everything in the first days, gives again in the inauguration of the Kingdom. The outpouring of His mercy in response to the soiled creation is through the seed of the woman. The incarnation of the Son, Jesus of Nazareth, is the ultimate gift to an undeserving people. He came and gave of Himself. In the end (or perhaps the New Beginning) He offered himself as the ultimate sacrifice on the cross for the sake of the whole world. He saw it coming the entire time. Jesus gave the gift that was necessary to reconcile not only humans, but also the entire world back toward the way it was supposed to be.

RESPONDING TO GIFTS

How does receiving a free gift make us feel? Does it cause us to cringe? Do we become calloused to this gift given millennia ago? Do we feel a sense of guilt and shame? Does the death of the Innocent One for the sake of the guilty elicit from us the same response Katniss had in the face of Peeta's gift? Perhaps this is the Achilles heel of the church in 21st century America. Generally speaking, we are a people who have a difficult time accepting free grace. For some it might even keep them from the goodness of the gospel. The good news is good precisely because Jesus' work on the cross is a work we cannot do, but it must occur to bring wholeness to God's distorted world.

Years ago, as a young campus minister, I trained with other first-year staff. Together with our mentors, we walked through our experiences on campus and discussed the ways we were leading and serving students. While we usually began by debriefing our ministry and talking about best practices, our conversations often looked a bit more like therapy sessions than training. During one such time, my colleague Sylvia—one of the most driven and seemingly successful newbies in the room—began to weep. She expressed that throughout the first year she had realized that she was not good enough to do the work of ministering to college students. This hit me hard. If Sylvia, who worked harder and longer than anybody else in the room, might not be "good enough" to do the work of the gospel, how was I?

Bill, one of my mentors, looked at her with caring eyes. He said, "Sylvia, you will constantly feel not good enough until you understand the reality of the cross." At first this seemed so simplistic. He continued:

As Americans, we believe that nothing comes for free. Our culture has taught us to pull ourselves up by our bootstraps and grit our teeth. The cross is counter-cultural. It teaches that the gift of God is just that, a gift. He has given it to you. You don't deserve it. You never will. As you get older—a little wiser and a lot more humble—you will come to realize this more and more. The point of the cross is that we can't do it. If we could, then the gospel is nullified.

Bill had given us a perspective of storied living. Sylvia and the rest of us in the room had developed a sense of leadership not from the free grace of the gospel, but from the synchronization of the American narrative and a particular interpretation of the Bible.

This lesson has stayed with me for nearly twenty years. The cross is the gift we cannot earn, the debt that no one can pay back. Nevertheless, we must respond.

> *Our response to the cross is the impetus for our leadership.*

It impels us into the challenges of faithfulness and stewardship. The gift never requires repayment. If it did, it would not be a gift, nor would it be grace. However, gifts always require a response.

Our response should ultimately be one of worship. Not only traditional spiritual engagement, but the gift also calls for worship that requires the laying down of our own bodies and our livelihoods in a spiritual act of worship. The only suitable response is one of sacrificial offering of ourselves and our lives.

DOWN FROM THE MOUNTAIN

There is another story, a much older one than Katniss' or Sylvia's, which has captured my imagination for many years now. It is the story referred to as the Mount of Transfiguration. Throughout Jesus' ministry, the disciples had given all to follow the Son of God—ministering with Jesus and observing His miracles. The scriptures teach us that it was a tedious journey of sacrifice, trials, and, at times, humiliation. While there were certainly glimmers of success, it was a hard life.

In the Gospel of Matthew, after the Pharisees and Sadducees tested Jesus, we read this:

> And Jesus went on with his disciples to the villages of Caesarea Philippi. And on the way he asked his disciples, "Who do people say that I am?" And they told him, "John the Baptist; and others say, Elijah; and others, one of the prophets." And he asked them, "But who do you say that I am?" Peter answered him, "You are the Christ." (Mark 8:27-29)

In the midst of the controversy over His identity, it was time to tell the disciples who He was and the purpose for which He had come. Even with this revelation, Peter challenges his Lord when Jesus tells them of his looming death. Peter is determined to save Jesus from His mission. Jesus responds: "Get behind me Satan!" (Mark 8:33).

Six days after this famous rebuke, Jesus takes His three closest disciples and climbs a mountain. The gospel writer tells us what happens next: "And he was transfigured before them, and his face shone like the sun, and his clothes became white as light" (Matthew 17:2). The disciples also saw Moses and Elijah—members of the great cloud of witnesses from the stories they had heard all of their lives—standing amongst them. Can you imagine seeing Jesus as He really is, as God himself?

Peter responds as he often does, by speaking his first inclination. He says, "Lord, it is good that we are here. If you wish, I will make three tents here, one for you and one for Moses and one for Elijah" (Matthew 17:4). Peter is granted a gift that none of us will experience before the return of the King. And he wants to stay. We can't blame him. In our moments of private or public worship—in the times when we feel the closest to the unseen God, we too want to remain. However, Peter's response is not the right one.

Instead of staying on the mountain, dwelling in the good presence of the Son and the fathers of the faith, Jesus leads the disciples down the mountain. When they get to the bottom, we discover the rest of the followers in a precarious situation. They are face-to-face with a demon-possessed boy and are unable to cast it out. Jesus arrives and heals the boy.

The lesson is clear: a true engagement with Christ is not one that impels us further into the prayer closet or moves us to remain within cloistered sanctuaries of the church. When we see Jesus as the Son of the Living God, we are not meant to stay away from the wearied world. Understanding Jesus and the gift of redemption drives us down from the mountain and into the wearied world. Seeing the Son must impel us toward service.

THE LEADER'S RESPONSE
As mentioned earlier, gifts do not require repayment, but they do elicit a response. This response shouldn't be

motivated by guilt and shame, or works-righteousness. We respond by going out into the world and working for its restoration. We work to create beautiful, useful, and healthy things. Through mountain-moving faith, we can make a difference in the fields to which God has called us.

In this story there are several critical things that the leader must understand. First, the gift of redemption is real and effective. Jesus paid the price of a humiliating death for all things on earth. This is a gift, and it is unearned. Second, the leader must spend time reflecting on the gift. While there was work to be done, Jesus took Peter, James, and John to experience His true identity. In similar ways, no matter how busy we become, we also must prioritize "seeing" Jesus, through reading His words and remembering His deeds. In this, we hear the echoes of the words of the Father. Third, in the end, we are not to hole up in that reflective experience.

The faithful leadership response is to return to the work of restoration and cultivation.

Parker Palmer explains that a "shadow among leaders is 'functional atheism,' the belief that the ultimate responsibility for everything rests with us. This is the unconscious, unexamined conviction that if anything decent is going to happen here, we are the ones who must make it happen—a conviction held by people who talk a good game about God."[2] We often believe, in the depths of our hearts, that it is through the works of our hands and through our power that we affect change. Although we acknowledge that the good work we do is by the grace and power of a world-creating God, this is often just lip service. We act as if we have the whole world in *our* hands—that we fail or succeed by our power.

To fight functional atheism, the leader must remain in communion with the Lord. We must continue up the mountain—in solitude and with others—as a way to be revived, reminded, and to relish in the God who loves us and the world. The daily return to the mountain, the constant focus on the work of Jesus should impel us to realize that the work we do is a response to hearing the call of the story and seeing the sacrificial Lamb. In this communion, we are reminded that the God who made us, who knows us, and who loves us, calls us to the fantastic adventure of leadership, not through the strength of our own hands, but through the power of the cross.

FOR DISCUSSION OR REFLECTION:

1. Think about or talk about the experience of receiving gifts you do not expect. Generally, what is your
   response? Why?

2. When you consider the notion that God's grace is given
   through Jesus' death and resurrection, how does this
   make you feel? Grateful or ashamed? Why?

3. Reflect upon ways that you can actively respond to this
   gift in your work, your life, and your corporate worship.

4. How does your thinking about your work as a response
   to God's gifts change your perspective on that work
   and your role in it?

CHAPTER 6
Faithfulness

Raising three young children means that our house is full of energy, toys, snacks, and noise—lots of noise. Although hard and tiring, it is one of my highest callings in the Kingdom. My role as a father is invaluable in the lives of my kids as I attempt to faithfully direct their young hearts and minds. One of the ways that my wife and I do this is through our bedtime routine and, in particular, our nightly prayers.

Each night we pray through the requests from our eight, five, and three-year-old. They are often mundane, and sometimes off-the-wall bizarre. They include petitions for sick friends, teachers, the babysitter, the stuffed animals, the rain, the scraped knees, the movie *Frozen*, and the dark. No matter what, we always conclude with this prayer: "Dear Jesus, give us wisdom to know what is right, and always give us the courage to do what is right even when it is hard."[1] Maybe you whisper a similar prayer at times. It is a reminder to continually seek what is good, true, and right—and to practice this even in the most difficult circumstances. This is an axiom that I want stuck in my children's minds at all times. Even though they are still very young, we have begun the practice of repetition through that prayer. This is a family liturgy.

I recently watched a moment of irony play out during one of our bedtime routines. I was with our youngest, trying to get him to stay in bed—a difficult feat in and of itself. A sudden commotion across the hall in the bathroom disrupted us. My oldest screamed in pain as I heard my wife utter words of disbelief. I walked into the bathroom, there stood Toby, holding his eyes and crying. He had sprayed the bottle of air freshener directly into his face. My investigation of the incident revealed that his sister had told him to do it. When I turned to Zoe she just shrugged her shoulders and gave a look that suggested, "Hey, don't look at me, he should know better."

The irony is that yes, he does know better. Toby knows that spraying anything in your eyes, especially a chemical, will bring about discomfort. And yet he couldn't resist. Even though we recite that prayer together every night, it was difficult to do what was right. It is the same with us. We all struggle at times with doing what we know is right.

For many years now, one of the most popular books on the topic of leadership has been *The Leadership Challenge*.[2] The authors explore what the best leaders do and how to make a difference in an organization. The title itself strikes a chord with many of us considering our own responsibilities in leading. Leadership is challenging. It comes complete with ups and downs, conflict, difficult decisions, and confusion. Due to the difficulty of leadership, I borrow from the title of that book when discussing the importance of fidelity in regards to our work. We could call it the faithfulness challenge.

WHAT IS FAITHFULNESS?

If I asked you to use faithful in a sentence you might say something like: "He is certainly a faithful friend," or maybe, "My grandparents have been faithful to each other for over forty years," or you might go with, "I'm faithful to my (insert hometown sports team) forever!" From these examples we would think of things like commitment and loyalty to relationships, institutions, and places. We must also grasp a more complete understanding of faithfulness to lead well.

Author Max De Pree, writing about what an organization needs from its leaders, writes, "At the heart of fidelity lies... promise keeping."[3] A leader does not make promises that she cannot keep. One of the surest ways to lose the trust of your followers is for them to see a lack of follow-up to your commitments. De Pree later writes, "Truth telling is at the heart of faithfulness." Similarly, the trust of your followers rests on them having confidence in things that you tell them. Communicating the truth, even when it is hard, and sticking to all of your commitments exemplifies the faithful leader. These are non-negotiable for leaders, whether you are leading with a title or exhibiting unlabeled influence in a community. It's hard to lead for very long if you are not being truthful, or if your follow-through is lacking. Practicing faithful leadership must include truth telling and promise keeping.

At its core, practicing faithfulness is the consistency of holding fast to what is good and true and doing it. But what does this entail? To provide a framework, consider four different aspects: the call to faithfulness we find in the scriptures, the necessary bedrock of personal character, the commitment that faithfulness requires, and consistency.

CALLING

There is a call to faithfulness. We see it exhibited in the fruit of the Spirit, "But the fruit of the Spirit is love, joy, peace, patience, kindness, goodness, faithfulness, gentleness, self-control; against such things there is no law" (Galatians 5:22-23). Luke makes it clear that we have a responsibility when it comes to faithfulness:

> One who is faithful in a very little is also faithful in much, and one who is dishonest in a very little is also dishonest in much. If then you have not been faithful in the unrighteous wealth, who will entrust to you the true riches? And if you have not been faithful in that which is another's, who will give you that which is your own? (Luke 16:10-12)

There are also the encouraging, yet blunt, words found in the book of Proverbs, reminding us that: "A faithful man will abound with blessings, but whoever hastens to be rich will not go unpunished" (Proverbs 28:20). And finally, the Apostle Paul's direct approach: "This is how one should regard us, as servants of Christ and stewards of the mysteries of God. Moreover, it is required of stewards that they be found faithful" (I Corinthians 4:1-2).

The scriptures are filled with verses similar to these, as well as stories about heroes of the Christian walk exemplifying faithfulness throughout their journeys. Moses led a confused people through the wilderness. Joshua remained steadfast in difficult situations. Jeremiah struggled for 40 years. Each of them answered the call to live faithfully in each of their spheres of influence. Make yourself familiar with these stories and draw hope from them regularly.

CHARACTER

Our personal character must be taken into account and developed in order to hold fast to what is good, true, and right. Faithfulness requires integrity—an integral wholeness. Does this mean that perfection is required? Hardly. If that were the case then no one could be considered faithful. Even the heroes just mentioned had their own flaws. Our original design, however, was one of perfect wholeness. Due to the Fall we are fragmented and distorted, yet the design remains. With the help of the Holy Spirit and the community of the saints, we strive toward less fragmented lives.

Integrity is living out of our fundamental assumptions and our core convictions. Faithfulness happens when we live with integrity. Author Robert Banks writes, "For character to take root, a person must first have principles, and principles must form into habits."[4] As our habits of the heart are lived out and practiced, we will begin to see the manifestation of faithfulness.

Leaders are able to live a life of liturgy;
they embed their core convictions into their daily lives.

This is integral living. David Greusel, an architect in Kansas City, Missouri, founded his own firm and thoughtfully named it Convergence Design.[5] Listening to David talk about his firm is to listen to someone describe a beautiful picture of integral living. The concept of convergence is that of bringing things together, of bringing things into a holistic picture of reality. This is how David lives his life and operates his firm. He believes that faithful living is about "bringing work, family and community together into a seamless whole." David has decided to be intentional about the way he lives his life. He exemplifies a narrative approach to leadership by considering the bigger story at play and how it influences his various habits of the heart. He has committed to a habit of the heart.

Henry Cloud describes character as "the ability to meet the demands of reality."[6] This is powerful and important because we face reality every single day. Reality is tough. Steve Garber writes that "the world is a hard place to live, but there is nowhere else to live."[7] How true. Faced with the difficulties of this place we call home, the harshness of this world is real for all of us. Cloud's statement then raises the question, is our internal makeup strong enough to face these realities? Faithfulness gives us the ability to meet the demands of reality. Thriving leaders have the character to meet these demands. It is difficult, yes. We often echo the cry of the hurting father from the Gospel of Mark, "I believe; help my unbelief!" (Mark 9:24).

COMMITMENT

The faith tradition I adhere to has historical roots in a group that is known as the Covenanters. Their story dates back to the 16th and 17th centuries during a tumultuous time of unrest in England and Scotland. King Charles I ruled over England, Scotland, and Ireland, and sought to establish his authority not only over the state, but also over the church. The great majority of the Church in Scotland held to the belief that Christ was head over all. Christ ruled over the state through the king and ruled over the church through the elders. While swearing humble allegiance to the king as he ruled over the state, these faithful followers refused to acknowledge that any earthly king had authority over the church; they would only acknowledge Christ as their head. The Church in Scotland wrote two major covenants articulating their position.

The king despised these covenants, persecuting, imprisoning, and often killing those who held to them. Over time, the majority of the Scottish population fell in line with the established church and renounced the covenants. They acknowledged the authority of the king of England over the church. However, a small group held fast to the belief that Christ was King and refused to renounce the covenants. They suffered for it. This small group became known as the Covenanters and practiced a difficult faithful response in the face of persecution. This commitment resulted in a denomination that is now over 350 years old.

Friedrich Nietzsche, "The essential thing 'in heaven and earth' is that there should be a long obedience in the same direction; there thereby results, and has always resulted in the long run, something which has made life worth living."[8] Eugene Peterson picked up on Nietzsche's line, writing a book entitled *A Long Obedience in the Same Direction* that captured the core of discipleship. This concept of long obedience in the same direction is fascinating. It is an essential aspect of fidelity. Our commitment to tasks at hand, people we influence, and the spheres in which we operate is necessary. The journey is long. In a world of instant access to worldwide information, minute clinics, and fifteen-minute car insurance quotes, long-term commitments seem counterintuitive. Faithful responses required in your leadership will at times be difficult and ordinary. The commitment will be hard when the latest trend passes or responsibilities become boring.

I really enjoyed watching the sitcom television show *The Office*. I've come to love how it epitomizes the everyday American workplace. So many times I've caught myself thinking: "No way would that ever happen in real life. Or could it...?" And then, "Yeah, it probably has." This is why the writing for this show is so brilliant. It brings to light those moments of everyday life—capturing insightful life lessons through the mundane work of a paper company. When the time came, my wife and I tuned in for the series finale with excitement. I enjoyed it, laughed, and then the last two and a half minutes completely captured me. One of the main characters, Jim, looks straight at the camera in the documentary-style of the show and reflects on his twelve years of working at a boring, yet wonderful job selling paper—something that, in the end, meant so much to who he has become. This is immediately followed by his wife Pam reflecting on the initial weirdness of a documentary crew following an ordinary paper company, she believes now in hindsight that it was a great idea. The entire show ends with Pam making one last simple insight, "There's a lot of beauty in ordinary things. Isn't that kind of the point?" Yes, it certainly is.[9]

I continually remind myself to practice the beauty of ordinariness through things like patiently brushing my daughter's hair, thoughtfully completing a year-end report that no one may read, responding to emails that may not necessitate a response, holding a sick child, weeding my garden, listening—really listening—to a colleague, and working through spelling words with my children. These are ordinary things that I feel a deep sense of calling to, a calling that necessitates faithfulness to each and every one of them. Take a moment right now to consider your own callings that may feel mundane. Be thankful for these and recommit yourself to them.

CONSISTENCY

There are three simple words over the door of my office. As every student and staff member exits they see: "on. off. after." I picked up this simple concept from a colleague years ago, and have used it ever since.[10] Small reminders are necessary to remaining consistent in our lives and leadership. These ten letters remind us that leadership is not just a life accessory, but a deeply engrained aspect that permeates our entire integrated lives. While I believe this is useful in many situations, let me explain how we talk about it in the context of student leadership development.

"On" is straightforward enough. When you are on the clock, your leadership is necessary and essential. Wherever you lead, you're on the job or in the spotlight. Whether you are a club officer, a resident assistant on your campus, the tennis captain, or a teaching assistant, these positions require you to take your influence seriously while serving. Whether it is the dining hall, the athletic field, your residence hall, or the classroom, you are representing yourself as a leader and at the end of the day, you are representing your institution.

The concept of "off" is where we really face the faithfulness challenge. Your influence is just as powerful when you are *off* campus or off the clock. Whether at Applebee's, on Facebook, or walking through your local community, you are exhibiting your influence. Someone is watching you. Influence happens even when it is inconvenient, even when you don't feel like leading. Consistency builds upon our commitments, the integrated life must exhibit multifaceted faithful leadership when we're "on" *and* when we're "off." In actuality, there is no true "off" for the Christian leader.

Finally, we must consider the importance of "after." Even now you are preparing for future opportunities. I always make it clear to students that I care deeply about their leadership development. Their preparation to lead well in the various spheres of influence throughout their lives is crucial. It will affect all aspects of their life. College leadership opportunities provide a safe place for learning and practicing healthy and faithful influence. It is a leadership lab. Take full advantage of the opportunities you find yourselves in, seek the advice of trusted mentors, and practice your leadership.[11]

Faithfulness includes consistency in all of life's callings. In order to hold fast to what is true and good and right we must persist and, as the scriptures reminds us, "Run with endurance the race that is set before us" (Hebrews 12:1). Consider your leadership a journey that requires a marathon pace instead of a sprint.

BUT THIS IS SO HARD!

My love for action films draws grief from a few of my friends. Okay, so I'm a huge fan of movies filled with explosions and completely unrealistic physical feats. The *Mission Impossible* series ranks up there with some of my all-time favorites. There is a line that gets repeated in every film, as well as the old television series on which the movies are based: "Your mission, should you choose to accept it..." You also have a mission. The Christian leader embraces the call to faithfulness and accepts the challenge.

Embracing faithfulness has a support structure. Our faithfulness is rooted and held firm in God's perfect fidelity.

We accept this faithfulness challenge with the knowledge of His everlasting and faultless faithfulness.

The depth of Jeremiah's struggle in Lamentations is apparent, but it results in one of the most inspiring promises that we find in the scriptures. He writes, "The steadfast love of the Lord never ceases; his mercies never come to an end; they are new every morning; great is your faithfulness" (Lamentations 3:22-23). God is perfectly faithful.

We can also consider the awestruck psalmist and echo, "Your steadfast love, O Lord, extends to the heavens, your faithfulness to the clouds" (Psalm 36: 5). God is perfectly faithful. We can resonate with the promises of Psalm 89 that are filled with exhortations of God's faithfulness, including the proclamation: "Righteousness and justice are the foundation of Your throne; steadfast love and faithfulness go before You." God is perfectly faithful. Finally, the comforting words from Paul remind us that "not all have faith. But the Lord is faithful. He will establish you and guard you against the evil one" (II Thessalonians 3:3). God is perfectly faithful.

We have the hope and assurance that our faithfulness is always grounded in the fact that God is faithful. Leadership is hard. But this is the Kingdom story; this is the co-mission we are summoned to, in participation with the Creator Himself. *Storied Leadership* requires our faithful response—what an exciting adventure to join.

FOR REFLECTION AND DISCUSSION:

1. List your current on, off, and after responsibilities. Identify potential challenges in each of these areas. How will you continue to be faithful—on, off, and after?

2. I have found it helpful to draw a picture that depicts my many areas of faithfulness. Find your own way to do this and then reflect on it. Are there areas in your picture that need particular focus right now?

3. How will you continue on the long road of obedience? In other words, what would help you become more consistent in your faithfulness?

CHAPTER 7

Proximate Leadership

W hite Christmas lights glimmered in the college chapel as the student leaders put the finishing touches on the décor. Surrounded by a selection of beautiful hors d'oeuvres, the string duet tuned their instruments. The gifted guest speaker thumbed through her notes in anticipation of the big event. Everything was thoughtfully designed. The execution was coming together flawlessly. Prepared to usher a flood of people to their seats, the students opened the doors. In the end, almost no one came.

Everyone has an area of influence in which we lead. I've worked with young adults within higher education all of my vocational life. From campus ministry to residence life to outdoor leadership to the classroom, the call to develop young Kingdom-minded leaders who are able to dream big and work tirelessly has captivated me. The privilege of this work is often overwhelming. Motivating students to be fully engaged in their college experience is sometimes difficult. However, more often than not, young adults are marked by vigor and a vision that outpaces those of us who have worked in the trenches for decades.

Leading doesn't usually turn out like it does in the movies. We don't always hit the buzzer-beating basket and the hero doesn't always get the girl. No matter how diligent we are, no matter how charismatic we might be, and no matter how many leadership books we read, things do not work the way we expect them to—or the way they ought.

Working in higher education, we continually see friends struggle with the transition into life after college. Students leave with the hopes of transforming the world for the Kingdom of God as engineers, teachers, and social workers. They are given the trite commencement pep talks:

"Dream big!"
"Be someone special."
"You can change the world!"

Rather than seeing the world transformed through the application of all that they learned, they hit the wall and find disappointment. We see this in our work too, don't we? Cutting edge outreach programs fall flat, our supervisors lack vision for change, and the students in our Bible studies don't end up having their eyes opened to the transformational possibilities of the scriptures. I have walked with many students and friends through disappointments in life, love, and leadership.

MAKE PEACE WITH THE PROXIMATE

This book began with a rehearsal of the story of the scriptures. In shorthand, it is often talked about as Creation, Fall, Redemption, and Restoration. God created a perfect world, filled with potential to be unfolded. Due to the sin of the first caretakers, the perfect creation was utterly distorted. By the life, death, and resurrection of the God-Man named Jesus, the entire creation will be restored from its groaning. Finally, we know that the fullness of restoration will not come to fruition until He comes again to make all things new.

In our affirmation of this, we affirm the words of 20th century mystic-philosopher Simone Weil, that we are in a world of gravity *and* grace—distortion *and* renewal. Stated another way, we live in a time that many call the "already, but not yet." Christ's life, death, and resurrection have already won the victory, but the battle is not complete. Things are still not the way they are supposed to be.

Leadership is hard. If the story is true, why should we expect otherwise? Life in the world of gravity and grace means that our collaborative effort for effective change will not work out in the best ways possible. Ever. So, how then do we proceed?

Steve Garber, has worked with students and leaders in the halls of power in what is, perhaps, the most powerful city in the world. He has spent most of his days trying to help make sense of life and love and leadership in a world marked by distortion and restoration. Confronted with the disenchantment of friends and students working in our nation's capital, he realized the need to help people understand the life of a leader in the world of gravity and grace. Drawing on thinkers, both ancient and contemporary, he developed what has become one of my mantras: "Make peace with the proximate."

"Proximate" is closely connected to the familiar word *approximate*. Approximate comes from the Latin *approximare*, to come near. Being approximate means to come close to the way something ought to be. It is a two-sided coin. On one side, the approximate misses the bull's-eye. On the other side, it is not an utter failure, it still hits the target. We must embrace the fact that things will never be the way they ought in the world of gravity and grace. Garber writes, "I am sure of this: the vision of the 'proximate' tethers us to the world that we all really live in. Wanting otherwise as we might, there is no other world in which we can be at home."[1]

Making peace with the proximate means that we accept the world as it is and hold realistic expectations.

So then, how does one make peace with the proximate?

AVOID CYNICISM
The path of the cynic is the easy path.[2] The cynic cries, "The world is broken, so what's the use?" This is so simple. Expecting the worst is a mark of the cynic. The cynic lives in the world of Murphy's Law where whatever can go wrong always will go wrong. Observing actions and choices of others, the cynic assumes the worst possible intentions. Cynicism drives one to be hopeless in a world that is groaning for redemption.

However, cynics are cynical for good reason; they come by it honestly. Peter Senge writes: "Scratch the surface of most cynics and you find a frustrated idealist—someone who made the mistake of converting his ideals into expectations."[3] Or to quote Alain de Botton, "Cynics are—beneath it all—only idealists with awkwardly high standards."[4] This is right. I know because it is true of me. Cynicism creeps in through years of living in the world of gravity and grace with an idealistic hope that things can be the way we think they ought and then seeing time and again the ought not coming to fruition. The cynic is most often born from a life of best intentions. Over the long haul, leaders let us down, followers let us down, institutions let us down, and we let ourselves down.

You see, the cynic has embraced a partial truth about the world. Cynics know gravity. They know the Fall. They know this for good reason—they have experienced it again and again. Author J.R.R. Tolkien, in a letter to his son Michael, explains, "The greater part of the truth is always hidden, in regions out of the reach of cynicism."[5] The father of Hobbits and Middle-earth is right on the mark. There are aspects of truth. In grasping after reality, partial truths can be ascertained. The cynic has grasped part of reality, but not the deeper, fuller truth.

Will things ever be the way they ought to be? No, not according to the Christian story. Not on this side of Paradise. Accepting the Fall and embracing grace means that we are always in a world of misdirection. Do we then reject the possibility of goodness? Absolutely not. There are always glimmers of God's grace. If we look hard enough, and acknowledge the creational goodness, we see that all things maintain aspects of the good, the true, and the beautiful. This is the deeper truth that Tolkien claims is outside of the grasp of the cynic. Cynicism is a disease to which we are all susceptible.

AVOID NAIVE OPTIMISM

Just as the cynic heartily embraces one side of the fall-redemption duality, so does the naïve optimist. He believes that no matter what, things are going to turn out just fine. The naïve optimist clings to the assumption that things will always go as planned, people will always show up, and mistakes will not be made—particularly in terms of his own work. In the story about the Christmas program, we had succumbed to naïve optimism. We had the best laid plans and we had worked tirelessly. Our team trusted that all would end well. If you have watched enough science fiction films, you know the line that so many of them begin with. Just as the scientists are about to mix the chemicals that will alter people into being super-strong or super-smart or super-(fill in the blank), they turn to one another and utter: "What could possibly go wrong?"

Whether we say them or not, as optimists, we live out these words. What could possibly go wrong? Well, in this post-Fall time, in the days of gravity and grace—sin and redemption—anything could go wrong. Better yet, nothing will go perfectly right. To ask what could possibly go wrong is a mark of the naïve optimist.

Granted, it is hard to find a self-attesting naïve optimist. Yet, as leaders, most of us are functional naïve optimists. That is, we attest, cognitively, that things might not work out the way we planned. Unlike the cynic, we seldom think that what could go wrong will. However, we most often operate out of the assumption that things won't go awry. Even more often, we are surprised when they do. This is the road to cynicism. We believe everything can be the way it ought, but time and time again it doesn't turn out that way. We are ground down by the hard realities of leading in a broken world (as broken people) and we lose hope that things could be better.

EMBRACE PROPHETIC LEADERSHIP

If neither cynicism nor naïve optimist is the way forward, how should we posture ourselves in the world of gravity and grace? The work of Walter Brueggemann offers hope as we live in a world of distortion and renewal. In *The Prophetic Imagination*, Brueggemann develops a perspective of the leader as prophet. He doesn't suggest that she is a seer or future teller, but rather someone who is able to see reality as it is, is deeply moved by the brokenness, and shapes a vision of a different, hopeful future.

How then do we embrace the posture of the prophetic leader in our practice? The prophet is akin to the cultivator and restorer mentioned earlier in the book. She is one who sees, remembers, and imagines. First, she *sees* the current state of affairs, the way things are. A prophetic leader does not try to sugar-coat the current reality, rather she pays attention and describes. She does not look at situations through rose-colored glasses. Rather, the prophetic leader shapes the people's perspective with the understanding that God's grace is in every situation—not with naiveté—but with the knowledge that the created order is always, no matter how bleak, mixed with kernels of goodness. She is a storied leader.

As we have already mentioned, Joshua, leading the Israelites into the Promised Land, instructed the people to build a monument as a catalyst for remembering God's goodness throughout the past wanderings. *Remembering,* and helping the people recall God's providence is a vital role of the prophetic leader. She builds perspective by remembering the goodness of the past as a way to assist living in the present and look toward the future. The scriptures are full of movements of remembering. Remembering is commanded—and for a good reason. When things get difficult, the remembrance of God's good providence shapes perspective and grants hope.

The prophet is able to *imagine* a different future and cast a vision to her people. Imagination is often misunderstood. We generally consider it as daydreams or the imaginary friend of a child. Brueggemann suggests that the imagination of the prophet is something altogether different. Whether wandering in the wilderness or feeling abandoned in exile, the people of Israel believed that the things of the present—the status quo—were the way things would remain. Cynicism creeps in and positive change seems impossible. This sounds all too familiar to many of us. Whether during crises at our colleges or simply through the numbing effects of the mundane, it is easy to believe that things will not change.

Standing in the midst of a community overwhelmed by the status quo, the prophet has the ability to shape what Brueggemann considers visions of alternative future realities that break the numbness of the status quo.[6] Leading in a world of gravity and grace involves understanding the present condition, remembering the goodness of God and the story of redemption, and casting a vision of alternative future realities—realities marked by hopeful expectation.

PROPHETIC LEADERSHIP ON THE GROUND

Two years ago I transitioned from directing an office in student affairs into a faculty position in our Master of Arts in Higher Education program at Geneva College. Currently, the program is celebrating its twentieth year of service. It has nurtured and developed hundreds of professionals in the field—literally influencing tens of thousands of students. Several of our alumni are now deans at their institutions and we expect to see our influence continue to grow. God has been very good to us.

After two years of teaching, I have been commissioned to direct this program. Taking the baton, I turned my eyes to the future and began dreaming what we could become going into our next twenty years. Like many institutions similar to ours—small, faith-based, and tuition-driven—we have entered a precarious time as tuition increases and the economy falters. The question of the value of private higher education is at its height. Meanwhile, local and national programs like ours continue to develop. Competition in the "marketplace" is on the rise. In the face of this climate, upper level administration has announced the beginning of a difficult process to consider the possibility of cutting academic programs.

Uncertainty about the future looms. I learned that a faculty member with significant teaching load is moving on from the institution. I find myself leading a renowned program at an institution that is looking to make cuts. See where this is going?

The work of this book is not merely theoretical. We aren't dealing with abstraction, disconnected from real life. The rubber meets the road every day, and we attempt to lead toward positive change. I have choices to make, just like you. With new difficulties on the horizon and resources dwindling, it is easy for me to become the cynic. I could sit by the rivers of Babylon and weep, believing that the status quo will always remain. I could assume that the Fall wins—that future realities will be worse than the present. I could succumb to the disease of cynicism. We see this happen in educational leadership all of the time. We also see the naïve optimist, placing their heads in the sand with disregard for very real difficulties. Both are unfaithful responses.

At our celebration of twenty years of service equipping higher education professionals we gathered with current students and a handful of alumni. Stories were told of the good work done by my friend who was moving on. As I rose to address the group, I picked up this theme of story. I explained that in a time like this we must celebrate the stories of God's grace and remember His goodness in the past. We also need to deeply consider the present, that God has called us all into this institution's story and that we—faculty, staff, and students—are a crucial part of it. Most importantly, this is not our story. It's His. We work in a little corner of the Kingdom of God called Higher Education. It is in no way separated out from the realities of that story; it is deeply embedded in it.

Standing in a beautiful church, I chose to embrace neither cynicism nor naïve optimism, but rather prophetic hope. Acknowledging present realities, remembering God's goodness to us through the development of this little program, and casting a vision of an alternative future reality, I am trying to move forward in hope.

In all of this, Brueggemann encapsulates the prophetic leader as the one who embraces the dialectical acts of criticizing and energizing. He explains that more liberal Christian traditions spend most of their time criticizing the status quo—speaking out against injustice and broken institutions. Conversely, conservatives energize the community toward a hope in a loving God that cares for his creation and image bearers, but tend not to criticize their current contexts. The former can tend toward cynicism, the latter naïve optimism. Prophetic leadership is never epitomized by one or the other, but always by both. Criticizing where we are and energizing toward a future hope, the prophetic leader makes peace with the proximate, she casts a vision and leads toward what might one day be.

Making peace with proximate leadership enables us to acknowledge the Fall without being enslaved by cynicism. It finds hope that is not unknowingly idealistic. Knowing the story, the able college leader embraces God's grace that is never manifested through cynicism nor naïve optimism.

FOR DISCUSSION OR REFLECTION:

1. Think about or talk about something about your current reality that is terribly difficult. Can you see both aspects of gravity and grace in the situation?

2. In your life and leadership, are you someone who is more of a cynic or naïve optimist? How do you see this manifesting itself?

3. How does a consideration of proximate leadership affect you? Does it bring you hope? Can it reshape your perspective?

CHAPTER 8
Called as Stewards

What comes to mind when you hear the word "stewardship?" Many immediately think of balancing a checking account and tithing to a local church. Maybe your thoughts went directly to your neighborhood park and the annual cleanup you do there. Very good things, but as you'll see, stewardship goes beyond these. Storied leadership is faithful stewardship of all of the things that God entrusts to you.

THE RESPONSIBILITY
We will start with the responsibility of stewardship involved in leadership. Stewardship is one of our inescapable calls. Let's back up and make sure we understand the bigger picture. An adequate understanding of *vocation* is necessary. After all, our leadership and stewardship fit into the idea of vocation. Parker Palmer wrote, "The deepest vocational question is not 'What ought I to do with my life?' It is the more elemental and demanding 'Who am I? What is my nature?'"[1] These are deep fundamental questions that we all wrestle with. It starts with an

understanding of our design as *Imago Dei*—we are God's image bearers. It is our responsibility then to continually practice "image bearing" in all that we do. How does this get us to a better understanding of vocation?

The terms *vision* and *vocation* saturate the Old Testament and New Testament. *Kalein* is Greek for calling. It means either "to name," "to invite," or "to summon." These concepts often coincide. *Kalein* primarily comes down to two things. First, it is an invitation to join the members of the people of God and to take up the duties that pertain to that membership. These are the two greatest commandments—to love God and love neighbor—the general calling of all believers. Secondly, there are a variety of diverse and particular callings. These are special tasks, offices, or places of responsibility within the covenant community and in the broader society.[2]

Everyone has many "particular callings" to steward. Embracing our identity as *Imago Dei* we are agents participating in His Kingdom, contributing to whatever we are involved in and wherever He has placed us. James Davison Hunter writes:

> If, indeed, there is a hope or an imaginable prospect for human flourishing in the contemporary world, it begins when the Word of shalom becomes flesh in us and is enacted through us toward those with whom we live, in the tasks we are given, and in the spheres of influence in which we operate.[3]

A robust understanding of vocation means that we heed all of our various callings, practicing faithful stewardship with each of the various activities God has blessed us with.

The beauty of stewardship is that God entrusts us with His stuff. Think about that for a second. I get nervous when my kids play with my phone, let alone the rest of my belongings. Yet the Creator of all that is has decided that we should watch over His creation and take care of it. This calls for intentionality and faithfulness in all areas of our lives. God trusts us to carefully look after and care for everything that is His. And by the way, that's *everything*. In the first chapter of Genesis, we read that we were created in God's own image and instructed to be fruitful, to multiply, and to have dominion over all living things. As we continue to read we receive further explanation, "The LORD God took the man and put him in the Garden of Eden to work it and keep it" (Genesis 2:15). We are caretakers of creation.

Talking about stewardship with my students, I continually bring it back to the conversation about being stewards of our gifts and places. We all have unique God-given gifts that must be unwrapped, developed, and exercised. Additionally, we all operate within spheres of influence that require our attention. These two concepts are a fantastic starting point for our consideration of stewardship.

STEWARDSHIP OF GIFTS

Think about how many light bulbs there are in the world. They're in our homes, on the buildings we visit, in our handheld devices, on our streets, brightening the world around us. There are billions of these things. We typically give very little thought to the omnipresence of light bulbs in the Western world. While traveling recently, I was fascinated by the light bulb. Flying over a number of cities I was overcome by the fact that so many exist. Each casting its light as far as it can, until another picks up where the last one left off. Without these, darkness. Thanks to Edison, our world is lit by glass and filament.

Remember the old Sunday School song? *This little light of mine, I'm gonna let it shine. Let it shine, let it shine, let it shine.* Each of us exists with a light to shine. What does that mean? The words of Matthew's gospel come to mind. We are the light of the world, a city on a hill. This is not exactly our own light. It is the light of our Creator and sustainer continually shining in us and through us. Our light reveals His glory. It is part of our image bearing responsibility. The curse is found far and wide, and it's dark. But there are light bulbs throughout—shining in our communities, in our schools, in our homes and in our places of work.

Here's the other thing I began to ponder looking down on all those light bulbs from 30,000 feet. Inevitably, someone changes each one of those bulbs. It's act of stewardship to ensure that the necessary light continues to shine. So, are we called to care for our own lights? I think so. Our stewarding responsibilities begin with stewarding the *Imago Dei*—the gift of God's image, the One that we were created to reflect. Again, the first chapter of Genesis provides insight here, "So God created man in his own image, in the image of God he created him; male and female he created them" (Genesis 1:27). What does it mean to actually steward the image? First, image-bearing is not passive, it requires action. We must practice our image-bearing responsibilities day in and day out. We have already seen that this is done through cultivating the creation. In this, it is about loving God, and loving neighbor. It is an active pursuit toward the coming Kingdom. Second, and similarly, it is a daily denying of ourselves. The Gospel of Luke and Paul's letter to the Romans remind us to die to ourselves and walk not in the flesh, but in the Spirit. We also see in II Corinthians that we are to continually be transformed into the likeness of Christ. Remember that we are continually working toward operating according to our "kindedness." Our "kindedness" is that of an image bearer—a lord of creation, the likeness of God Himself.

How do we do this well? How do we continually conform to His image? Here is a list to get you started:

» Pray. We daily—hourly—seek the wisdom of our creator and sustainer. The very one whose image we are reflecting.

» Read. We continually rely on the illuminating Word of God to guide, instruct, and clarify our daily activities. Not only this, but we also must immerse ourselves in the great books of the faith, from the early church fathers to wise contemporary authors.

» Physical wellness. We take care of the physical body that God entrusts to us. It should be treated well with regular exercise, healthy food, and patterns of rest.

» Fellowship. We take joy in the membership of the body of believers.

Stewardship begins with caring for our light bulbs. It is important to care for the light that shines through us, lighting a dark world. Our image-bearing responsibilities require faithful stewardship of that very reflection.

THE GIFTS WE USE
In addition to the gift of God's image, each and every one of us is gifted with unique talents, strengths, skill sets, and abilities. These are the tools that God places in our hands in order for us to participate with Him in His mission in the world. Just as we look differently and exhibit diverse personalities, so too do we represent different talents— functioning as different parts of one body.

The strengths and abilities that have been entrusted to us also require faithful stewardship. When I work with students I will often use the words *discover* and *develop* regarding our leadership abilities. It is a process that is as true for the young as it is for the experienced. Theologian, statesman, and journalist Abraham Kuyper once wrote, "We must, in every domain, discover the treasures and develop the potencies hidden by God in nature and in human life."[4] Discovering and developing the potential that God has created within you is a critical task for leaders.

Discover
This discovering of our gifts can take on many forms. Self-awareness is the first step to knowing what gifts you have at your disposal. If we are unaware of the tools that we have available, then we are ill equipped to handle the leadership tasks we face.

My mechanic's name is Rick. When I take my car to the shop I see that the place is packed full of tools used to fix a variety of vehicles. The thing is, I myself wouldn't have the faintest idea as to what many of those tools are used for. That's why I'm there. I would need someone like Rick, who has spent decades discovering which tools are best utilized for certain repairs, to help me learn what each tool is used for. Learning about our own gifts, strengths, and skills is a necessary step toward fruitful leadership. Here are a few ways to begin discovering your gifts:

» Pray. It is always important to approach the discernment of our abilities by prayerfully seeking God's insight for those gifts he has blessed us with. Regularly ask God to show you those gifts. Pray for an open mind about certain gifts that you may even be hesitant about using.

» Assess. See if you can identify through journaling the things that you enjoy most and find satisfaction in. Simply make a list of the things you find great pleasure in and feel like you are "in the zone" when performing. Just considering what we're good at can go a long way.

» Seek. Ask those that you trust to give you honest feedback. Sit down with a mentor, a close friend, or a supervisor and ask them to point out certain skill sets that they see you exhibiting, or to tell you stories of when they saw you working most effectively. Some of these might surprise you.

» Survey. There are many instruments out there that can identify certain strengths, passions, and skill sets in our lives. Popular ones include: The Myers-Briggs Type Indicator, StrengthsFinder, The VIA Institute on Character Survey, and The Four Colors Personality Test. These are just a few instruments that I've found helpful over the years. These are not perfect diagnostic tools; they merely give us a language to use with others as we seek to understand our strengths.

To seek out and discover the gifts that each of us has is to practice good stewardship. This does not end after taking an assessment or two or asking somebody what we are good at. This is a lifelong process. We continue unwrapping gifts that God has given to us as we explore the depths of our intricate design. Our stewardship of gifts does not end here, however; we must shape and develop these strengths and abilities.

Develop
Have you ever attempted to learn how to play an instrument or become fluent in a different language? Maybe you are an athlete or an artist. How do you develop the skills required to do these things well? You practice. It is the same with your leadership.

You can develop your gifts most effectively by keeping three things in mind. First, learn something new about your gift. This is a little different than discovery. You may find that you have the gift of verbal communication, but taking a course about communication or watching TED talks in order to observe good communicators will teach you more about the gift. Second, you practice your gift. Let's stay with the example of communication. Find opportunities to actually perform small group talks on a regular basis. Spend time crafting presentations and figure out what works best for you when speaking. Third, you solicit feedback about your gift. Learn from others around you as they point out things that you do really well when talking, as well as things that you may need to work on. When you receive specific instruction regarding your gifts, practice your gifts day in and day out, and ask others to help you understand your gifts and improve on them, you intentionally develop the strengths and abilities that your leadership requires. This will allow you to steward your gifts even better.

Another key component of development is using our gifts to help others develop theirs. You may have heard the phrase, "The best way to learn something is to teach it." Similarly, our own gifts are developed as we help others cultivate theirs. Anjelica, a student of mine, describes her experience with student leadership training this way, "I am now excited to invest in someone who can potentially better our residence hall and campus. By investing in Taylor, I will grow as a leader while helping her grow as a new Resident Assistant."[5]

STEWARDSHIP OF PEOPLE & PLACES
When considering stewardship, it is important to think of the responsibility we have to our places. Recognizing the places and tasks that God has called us to and entrusts us with is imperative. The focus here is on the people and places influenced by our leadership within those spheres.

People
For leaders, your stewardship of place includes the people of that place. Another way to put it is to say that followers, those whom we influence, are also entrusted to our care.

As we lead and steward we must provide hospitable places that allow relationships to flourish.

We must have a robust understanding of what it means to steward the people we are leading.

I mentioned earlier that this idea of stewardship begins by faithfully bearing the image that we are designed to reflect. We are bearing the image of the Triune Godhead. God himself exists in community. It follows that we will better reflect the image of God when we work together in a flourishing community. An act of relational stewardship to participate in this flourishing community is required. Eugene Peterson writes:

> When we are in a community with those Christ loves and redeems, we are constantly finding out new things about them. They are new persons each morning, endless in their possibilities. We explore the fascinating depths of their friendship, share the secrets of their quest. It is impossible to be bored in such a community, impossible to feel alienated among such people.[6]

This is a beautiful picture of thriving human relationships. It does not happen, however, on a whim, or without deliberate action. A storied leader understands that each member of a community has a role to play and that it takes hard work to see the manifestation of a community like Peterson is describing. Seeing a community like this manifested, it takes the work of those who will lead in a way that makes it possible.

Places

There is a product line of household figurines that I am assuming many of you have seen at your local Hallmark store or may even have in your home. Willow Tree, represented by Kansas City-based DEMDACO, makes these faceless wooden figurines that have become the most popular creation of this home décor company. I had the privilege of visiting DEMDACO and talking with Dave and Demi Kiersznowski, the company's founders and owners. This husband-and-wife team approaches their business with more intentionality than I have seen nearly anywhere else. They have clearly made a decision to faithfully steward the organization and place that has been entrusted to their care.

Walking into the headquarters, your first feeling is one of hospitality. A warm reception area greets you. Its wall is adorned by a piece created by world-renowned Makoto Fujimura. His art is a thing of beauty that captures the essence of DEMDACO's vision. Moving through the building you learn more about the Kiersznowski's intentionality with place. The meeting rooms are named after what Dave and Demi call "heroes of the common good." You may have your morning staff meeting in the Mother Theresa room. You might attend a quarterly strategy meeting in a room honoring Dr. Martin Luther King, Jr. By late afternoon you may have a product launch brainstorm meeting in the William Wilberforce room. This room naming is a small gesture really, but it bursts with meaning and intentional stewardship of place.

When you arrive at the top floor you walk out into a large open common space. Our group ate in this room and listened to Dave and Demi talk about why they created that space the way they did. On a regular basis, DEMDA-CO's employees, along with their families, are invited to spend Friday evening hanging out in the common area. They put in a movie for the kids, fill the room with the smell of popcorn, and let the adults carry on with conversation and laughs. The Kiersznowskis understand the importance of caring for the people that are entrusted to them and an intentionally designed physical place to ensure that is no small detail.

DEMDACO is one small example, but this Kansas City company is a signpost of Christ's Kingdom. Their intentionality shows us what it can look like to take a place that God entrusts to us and care for it like He intends. Consider Dave and Demi's purpose statement for the company: "Pursue business the way it ought to be." There is an intended design for our places. We must care for them with this in mind. The stewardship of place goes beyond cleaning up after ourselves. It is about thinking deeply in regards to each of the places we operate within and approaching each with sincere thoughtfulness about how they are designed, how they work, and what they communicate.

What is it that we do to practice better stewardship of the places we are in? It is helpful to keep a few things in mind:

> » Identify. What are the needs of your local community? What are your current tasks? Where are your spheres of influence? Take inventory and identify the actual places that you can contribute to and care for. List all of these places.

» Commit. Stewardship is not a drive-through concept—it takes work. This work may last much longer than we originally anticipated. In an increasingly transitory society, a commitment to a particular place can feel counter-cultural. G.K. Chesterton wrote, "Men did not love Rome because she was great. She was great because they had loved her."[7] Lovingly commit to the places you have been charged with stewarding.

» Think Positively. Henry Cloud believes that part of our work as leaders is to steward the thinking that happens in our places. Keep in mind how your attitude affects those around you, for good or ill.

» Ask. What needs to be done for the common good to be manifest? Find people that are affected by the influence you have within a particular place— ask them questions.

» Anticipate. What will this place need to continue flourishing?

GRITTY REALITY

Kingdom leadership is faithful stewardship. Living consistently with this in mind is important. Remember that we have been commissioned to work with God in His mission to bring all things back into accordance with his original design. He is making all things new. Participating in the *Missio Dei* means that we are responsible caretakers of His world.

Speaking at a university commencement ceremony, author James K.A. Smith told a group of excited young college graduates, "Dreaming big is easy. The bigger challenge is to dream small...to deepen your embeddedness in the gritty realities of everyday life."[8] God has intentionally put each and every one of you in spaces and places in order to serve His purposes. He has given you strengths and abilities to accomplish these purposes. Your responsibility is to steward these gifts and places well as you serve in the gritty realities of everyday life.

FOR REFLECTION AND DISCUSSION:

1. At times we can start to think exclusively of future opportunities. What does it look like to steward in the present—in the places you currently influence?

2. We can often feel responsible with what we know about the world, but not equipped to respond. Identify one current reality that should be addressed—brainstorm with a friend or group to discover ways in which you could faithfully respond.

3. What particular strengths, gifts, and abilities do you have that need to be developed? Identify a way in which you will do that in the next six weeks.

Practicing the Story

Thus far we have discussed foundational concepts regarding leadership from a Christian perspective. These are essential elements for the Christian leader to grasp as he influences in his different roles. As we have identified the importance of the story of the scriptures and our various callings, we have held to an understanding that leadership is a process that takes healthy collaboration to accomplish purposeful change. As Kingdom collaborators it is important to know and remember the Kingdom story and how it shapes our leadership. It is from here that we faithfully serve in our roles as cultivators, restorers, and stewards.

What follows is a section entitled *Practicing the Story*. Even with the best of intentions, leading without purposeful action will accomplish very little. We must continually work out our leadership through daily practice and exercising our leadership muscles to avoid atrophy. We have compiled six short leadership practices. This compilation is not exhaustive. We hope that you add to it as you find things that work for your own leadership situations. These are simply some of the concepts that we have learned to continually practice in our own lives as we attempt to lead faithfully.

The difficulty in writing about leadership is that it is a phenomenon filled with complexities. The risk in a list like this is that it can turn something like leading faithfully into a formula. Kingdom collaboration is not something we can approach with a ten-step plan. It is a journey, one that we are on for the entirety of our lives. We are always learning more about ourselves, others, and God's world— hopefully making us better leaders as we travel. These are things that we have found helpful over the years. We hope that you do too.

PRACTICE 1

Vision

L eaders understand the importance of vision. Time and again they are captured by the potential realities they see in the world. Leaders have the ability to navigate the tension between their current circumstances and these potential realities and influence others to do the same. Earlier, we discussed God's intended design for the creation, that there is a way the world *ought* to be. For the Christian leader, a desire for the way things ought to be should be embedded in every vision.

My family and I recently moved to a different house. There were no major problems, but as with any new living space, it came with its challenges. I immediately saw things that I wanted to change in order to make the house our own. I began to envision what it could become. New light fixtures, paint certain rooms, update the wiring, change the landscaping, add a bedroom upstairs—the list quickly grew. In my enthusiasm, I thought that I might be able to finish the list over a weekend. Of course this was ridiculous thinking, but I was captured by the idea of what my house could look like and I was ready to make it happen.

A vision-casting process does not happen over a weekend. It takes time to realize, develop, communicate, and execute. Using this practice should be a regular practice for leaders. We are always in one or more of these phases of the vision process. Vision can be a daunting word, particularly for the young emerging leader, but it isn't only for Fortune 500 company boardrooms. The Christian leader carries out the vision process in her family, her friendships, and her community. All areas of influence are fertile ground for this process.

REALIZE THE VISION

Remember that leaders work to see what could be and should be as they navigate in God's creation. They survey the landscape of the times they are in and they are able to see it for what it truly is. As we see the world around us, we must see the *oughts* around us—those things that should be better than they appear. The ability to see positive alternative future realities is how we start to realize a vision is needed.

It may be a program under your direction needing energy, a relationship requiring reconciliation, or a supervisee wanting direction. Realizing possibilities in any given situation is the first step in the vision process. Keep your eyes open for these possibilities, listen to those around you for clues as to what might be needed, and continually pray for guidance in each of your spheres of influence.

DEVELOP THE VISION

It is one thing to realize that there are possibilities to be pursued, but then what? Visions without thoughtful intentionality can fade quickly, or even do more harm than good.

A healthy and successful vision requires work and cultivation so that it can take root and influence purposeful change. Make sure that you take the time to do this. It can be a difficult part of the vision process. It will take patience and focus, but without it, a vision may die before it even gets off the ground.

» You could begin by simply writing out your vision. What do you see as a potential reality? Write down what you believe needs to change about a particular situation.

» Begin to pray and think intentionally about this situation. Pray and discuss your vision with others that you trust, asking for honest feedback.

» Take inventory of the values that will be manifest through this new reality, and at the same time consider the costs of this new reality.

» You may also want to investigate previous situations that are similar to your own. What can you learn from these as you craft your own vision?

COMMUNICATE THE VISION

A leader uses clear and intentional communication to cast a vision. Similar to communicating expectations, leaders will only create more challenges for themselves if they fail to communicate their vision. Again, this does not have to be an intimidating presentation in front of hundreds of people. For some leaders, it will at times be a large presentation, but it can also be a brief inspiring talk to a small Bible study group, or a motivating talk with family about improving relationships.

Always consider the timing of when to share your vision. A well-timed vision cast is a powerful thing. If you have arrived at this point, you are already excited and ready for what could be—now capture others' imaginations with it. This also inspires collective buy-in for the vision. A shared vision is rare and invaluable in the process of creating positive change.

EXECUTE THE VISION

It is possible to realize a vision, fully develop it, and communicate it in an inspiring fashion. But without action it will not accomplish change—which is at the heart of leadership. The leader that casts the vision must also live out the vision. To see change, one must act. Leadership is about modeling the way for others to follow in order to influence change.

This is a difficult part of the vision process. Remember that the faithfulness journey is a long road. Living out our visions is not always a quick realization of new realities. Some of them will take a long time and will need continual reminders of the vision that is guiding you along the way.

REMEMBER THE VISION

We have spent significant time exploring the power and importance of stories throughout this book. A vision is a particular story about the future—and it needs to be told over and over again. Just as the Israelites did as they wandered, agents of leadership retell the vision story to each other. Good remembering inspires hope and courage during the times when recalling the vision is difficult.

REVISIT THE VISION

It is okay to recalibrate visions. Leaders embrace the fact that they often face ever changing environments. Remember my house? The vision I have for it continues to change even now. As we make certain changes to the house, we begin to see more of its character revealed and we adjust the vision, even slightly, in order to create a more robust picture of what it will be like someday. We must also deal with setbacks, mistakes, and distractions as we work out the vision for our house. A leader understands that visions are not executed in a bubble. They learn to adjust and maintain a focus on the vision.

FOR DISCUSSION AND REFLECTION:

1. Where do you see different ways of doing things right now? Is there an area of your life where you see something that could be and should be?

2. Maintaining a vision is difficult. How will you remain committed to your visions?

PRACTICE:

1. Identify a vision for a current situation that you are influencing. Talk this through with someone you trust and write down how you are going to develop it and communicate it with those you are leading.

2. Spend 15 minutes this week in prayer, specifically asking for wisdom regarding specific visions that you are contemplating.

PRACTICE 2
Networking for the Common Good

Networking is generally understood as making initial connections within a sphere of work that are intended for the sake of future opportunities. While common definitions of networking tend to be relatively innocuous, I have always considered it a bit of a dirty word. It has always conjured images of sweaty businessmen in bad suits indiscriminately throwing their business cards around the conference room of a Holiday Inn. With the development of social media, I began to see it as shameless self-promotion on Twitter, Facebook, and LinkedIn. In my mind, the internet has become a virtual Holiday Inn where the businessmen no longer needed their bad suits. Their targets are a click away. Networking, in my mind, was always about using others to get ahead.

My preconceptions of networking all changed the day my best friend and admired colleague told me that he saw himself primarily as a networker. To my horror, I suddenly pictured Scott pressing sweaty palms and tweeting in his pajamas. My world turned upside down. A storied perspective requires a paradigm shift regarding our understanding of networking. Assuming that networking is inherently bad goes against my understanding of the narrative of the scriptures. We have gone to great lengths making the case that the world is made, in its entirety, to be good. Although everything is distorted by the Fall—God has an intended design for all things in His creation. My past consideration of networking was the response of the cynic shaped by negative experiences.

NETWORKING IS LOVING THE BODY

We are all image bearers of God. We share a common "kindedness" that is manifest in our propensity toward worship, our call to work, and our communal nature (among other things). Yet, we are also exquisitely diverse. Every human has a different story—their own perceptions of and experiences in the world. Each and every image bearer has different sets of gifts with varying configurations.

The apostle Paul writes about the church in terms of the body. We learn that all image bearers are different. Each has unique gifts at their fingertips. The body metaphor tells us that we cannot go it alone. We need each other. If we are all a different part of the body and the whole must work together, then networking is the sinews and tendons of the body. The network is an essential component of the body, connecting each part to the others. It is an essential aspect of Kingdom collaboration.

A reconsideration of our perspective on networking leads to a reorientation of our practices of networking:

OFFER MORE THAN YOU ASK

No part of the body is a parasite. Each needs something and has something to offer. As you enter a network, you must understand that you are a contributor, not just a beneficiary. This requires reflection and self-awareness. A simple rule of thumb is to offer more than you ask. Working well as a body in a community means that we will be known as contributors, not just askers.

CREATE VALUE

Earlier in the book I told the story about my guitar-building friend Patrick. He is a creator, restorer, and fine-tuner. So are you. Networking is easier when you create value for others and people see that value. This is not to say that networking is simply an exchange economy, but I have found time and time again that people want to invest in value creators. In general, people are not stingy. Leaders desire to invest in and share with other creators, restorers, and tuners. They see it as a wise stewardship of what they have. Contribute to your community, and others, for the most part, will be eager to contribute to your work and development.

YOU GOT NO

I have always been sheepish about asking for things. In ways, it is due to my hesitancy of seeming opportunistic. I am also simply afraid to be told "no." Talking about the possibility of asking for resources, my friend Greg looked at me and said, "As my grandma always said, '*No* you have, *yes* you can get.'" I was clueless as to what this meant. He explained that if you don't ask, the answer, by default, is no. Asking creates the possibility of a "yes." While a bit out of context, we can consider the words of James, "You do not have, because you do not ask" (James 4:2). Many times, in our work and lives this is true. We shouldn't resist asking out of fear of rejection or seeming opportunistic. Ask, be okay with "no," and deeply appreciate the "yes."

CONNECT FOR THE GOOD OF OTHERS

My friend Scott is a master networker. While many network for the sake of themselves, Scott understands that the thick network that God has given him is a gift that he must steward for the Kingdom. Whenever I talk with Scott about a project he says, "You should talk to so and so about this. Want me to make an introduction?" He understands that God has placed him in a particular place at a particular time to help people be successful. Scott does not do this out of any sort of selfish ambition; rather, he loves to see people helping others. Consistently connecting others for their sake has built thick relational capital for him. There are many eager to assist in his work.

This is simple, but incredibly hard. Connecting others is a practice I attempt to embody whenever I am talking with someone about their work. It takes listening and also considering if I have helpful connections to offer.

LOOK FOR OPPORTUNITIES

When I travel, I always consider people to connect with. This past year, while visiting my mother in South Carolina, she asked if I wanted to visit a small private Christian college near her home. I was intrigued by the institution as it had gone through some similar difficulties our institution has.

She set up a time to walk the campus and visit the art museum with her friend who is the curator there. To our surprise, her friend planned a tour that included meeting with the interim president and several directors. It was a fabulous time to develop a better network.

A few months later, I was visiting friends in Chattanooga, Tennessee. One of our students is a graduate assistant in athletics at Covenant College. I had never met the Athletic Director and staff, so I sent a quick email and asked for a meeting. While my family swam, I slipped out for a few hours to connect with these colleagues. In the end, I heard stories of their good work and talked about possibilities for additional positions in the future. By sacrificing two hours of a week-long vacation I had the opportunity to develop a thicker network. I expect this meeting will lead to ways for us to serve one another.

One of the best books on networking is *Never Eat Alone*, by Keith Ferrazi.[1] Ferrazi explains that we always have opportunities to connect with others. Possibilities to network are all around.

If you are a leader, I assume that you are a busy person. But even busy people need to eat. A way to develop a stronger network is to look for simple ways to connect with others. Could you make it a point to invite someone on your campus weekly for meal at the dining hall? It's easy. Take that time to get to know that person and let them get to know you. Talk about the projects that you are working on. It might not be for the sake of asking for something. In fact, it probably should not be. But it's a chance to develop a network through which you could serve one another in the future.

FOLLOW UP
Always, always, always follow up with someone with whom you have networked. Whether it was connecting someone with another person, a simple meet and greet, or a person that helped you to advance a cause, follow up with a correspondence thanking them.

It could look like any of the following:

» "Dr. Phillips, thank you for sharing your lunch hour with me. I enjoyed hearing about the way you designed your class on civic engagement. It was particularly helpful to get a picture of what developing local partners looks like."

» "Heather, I'm glad we had a chance to grab coffee at the conference. It was exciting to hear about your work with community partners. Here is a book I read recently that I thought you might find helpful."

» "Mr. Sanders, I really loved our conversation about the contours of young adult ministry at your church. Not sure if you're interested, but my friend is working on a project regarding race and evangelical young people. If you'd like I would be happy to make an introduction."

» "Donna, I just finished your book on community. I loved it! I particularly was struck by the chapter on connecting with people who are marginalized by strong communities. Thank you for your work. It means a lot."

A quick response, in a timely manner, will help to reinforce a network and move toward future connection.

By moving past our negative assumptions about networking, we connect our stories with others. Through these connections we can shape relationships that not only can be helpful in future work, but are also enjoyable and life-giving.

FOR DISCUSSION OR REFLECTION:

1. What have your experiences been like with networking?

2. What are some experiences you have had with making more significant connections with others? Can you identify what made the experience beneficial?

3. As you think of the community of the church as a body, what part of the body are you? What do you have to offer others? What are you lacking that could be provided by other members?

PRACTICE:

1. This week, think of someone that you would like to have as a part of your network. Invite them for lunch or coffee. Spend time learning about them, their passions, and the work they do.

2. Think about a recent conversation with someone about a project that they are working on. Consider a way that you can help them in their work. Send a short email pointing them toward a resource, offering a connection with a friend, or simply encouraging them of the importance of their endeavors.

3. While it might be uncomfortable, ask someone this week to help you in your work. It could be requesting someone to speak at a function, proofreading your writing, or requesting resources that could aid in your Kingdom work.

PRACTICE 3
The Expectation Gap

L eaders tend to like a certain amount of control when it comes to their area of influence. This is not always bad. Leaders are the ones who have stepped up, assumed responsibility, and decided to work toward change for the common good. Frustrations and discouragement along the way are inevitable.

On the path of my own leadership journey, I have found that frustrations often emerge due to a difference in expectations. It happens with supervisors, friends, parents, and neighbors. It's actually hard to find a place in the world where expectations and experiences are not misaligned. Often, we don't even realize that we had initial expectations, finding ourselves frustrated without even knowing why. Something seems missing between what we thought was going to happen and what actually happened. Let's call this the expectation gap.

Andy Stanley identifies it as the "gap between what we expect people to do and what they actually do."[1] As leaders, we decide what fills this gap. According to Stanley, we will choose one of two responses—believe the best or assume the worst. When your partner does not turn in her component of the group project, believing the best means that you decide that she had the best of intentions with getting the work done, but that a circumstance outside of her own control kept her from doing so. To assume the worst means that you quickly jump to judgment and decide that she disregarded the work because it was not important to her. Stanley asserts that the decision to believe the best is rooted in an organization's culture of trust—and leaders are responsible for establishing this environment.

What do you do when your experiences collide head on with your expectations? How will you establish expectations that are clearly understood in your arenas of influence?

WHEN REALITY HITS

There is a reoccurring story that I hear when talking with young professionals in my field. It goes like this: "I was so excited to start this new job. The campus and the people here are great. The first few weeks were busy, but I'm enjoying the work that I get to do. At this point I'm struggling with my supervisor; I don't understand what she wants from me. I feel like we're on different pages." As these conversations continue, I realize that these young leaders are facing an expectation gap. The honeymoon phase is over, reality has hit, and the job is not what they were imagining it would be like.

These are discouraging times. They elicit judgment and cynicism, and they can easily tempt us to just quit and walk away. If we walked away every time, though, we would never accomplish anything. So, how do we respond when we find ourselves in the gap?

1. Identify. Identify and acknowledge the gap between your initial expectations and what has now come to fruition in your experience. Simply stating that this has happened can begin to help. This is helpful to do alone, but even better if it can be done with all of the people involved.

2. Recognize Unmet Expectations. Evaluate these expectations. Which ones were not met?

3. Set New Expectations. Finding yourself in a gap does not mean the game is over. Take the time to recalibrate and adjust your expectations for moving forward.

AVOIDING GAPS

I teach an elective course for students pursuing a minor in leadership studies. I was excited to teach students who chose this course. However, by midterm, it seemed that very few of them wanted to be there and class discussion was anemic. One afternoon, I expressed my disappointment, letting them know that my expectations had been sorely unmet. A quiet, yet bold, reply from one of my students returned, "We didn't know that was what you wanted to see happen." I felt embarrassed. There I stood, proud of my ability to work in a "teaching moment" about the expectation gap, and I had failed to clarify those expectations.

Many expectation gaps in our lives can be avoided by communicating well with those around us. I could have bypassed a significant gap with my students had I stood up on the first day of class and clearly stated my excitement for robust discussion and anticipation for involvement. Were these expectations there? Of course, they were just not expressed. A leader understands the importance of clearing communicating what is expected. Leaders establish clear expectations for those whom are under their influence.

» Take Inventory. You need to know what your expectations really are. Some of these will always be consistent because of who you are and how you work. At times however, they will change with circumstances. Make sure you know what expectations you have for particular situations.

» Clarify. Leaders must learn how to communicate expectations with clarity. It is a necessary skill in leadership. Do this in writing whenever possible. If there are formal job descriptions, use them.

» Ask Others. The best leaders not only state their own expectations, but also ask others what their own expectations are. By sharing expectations up front, gaps are preemptively identified and avoided before it is too late.

» Check In. Just like regular car maintenance, our leadership journeys need regular check-in times. This includes expectation checks on a regular basis. Fix the gaps before they grow into canyons.

The expectation gaps in our leadership experiences can be devastating. Good leaders establish and communicate their expectations on a regular basis and know how to respond well when unexpected realities surprise them.

FOR DISCUSSION OR REFLECTION:

1. Do you remember a past experience that ended up being different than what you expected? Maybe it was a group project, a work experience, or a volunteer opportunity. Describe that time.

2. Are there particular people or situations that usually bring an expectation gap to the surface? What would it look like to start a conversation with that person? How could you avoid a gap with this situation in the future?

3. Is there a current situation that has you disappointed due to a difference from your initial expectations? What could you do to adjust your expectations moving forward?

4. This week, reflect on a past experience that resulted in an expectation gap—either due to your own expectations not being met, or due to someone else not clarifying expectations for you. What was that experience like? How did you respond? Journal ideas for handling situations like this in the future.

PRACTICE:

1. Identify at least three situations in your near future that need clear expectations to be established. What are they? Why is it important to have clear expectations for these?

2. Select one of these situations. Write out two clear expectations that you have for that particular situation. Practice communicating those expectations to a friend.

PRACTICE 4
Disarmingly Honest

Just one year out of college, I stepped onto the campus of Penn State University to work in campus ministry with the Coalition for Christian Outreach (CCO). It was a thrilling time of working with an amazing staff and a fabulous group of students. The CCO provided me with resources and a context to build a relatively successful ministry.

While the CCO facilitated mentors, connections, and training, one thing that they did not provide was a fully funded paycheck. I worked out of my 1988 Honda Civic hatchback and dined from the dollar menu. Campus ministry was invigorating. Raising support was not. My paychecks could attest to that.

In fundraising training I learned something that would not only affect my income, but more so, it would reshape how I lead. The trainer shared three words: "be disarmingly honest." While incredibly simple, we seldom practice disarming honesty. Often leaders believe that the way to influence effectively is to move strategically. For me, this meant trying to move others in a direction, often by indirect influence. This was never as Machiavellian as it might sound. I didn't go about lying and scheming. I was certainly honest, but not disarmingly so.

Several years ago I was working in the Center for Faith and Practice at Geneva College. In my position, we shared student discipleship coordinators with the college's residence directors. Most often, these partnerships were healthy Kingdom collaborations. At other times things were not all sunshine and rainbows.

At one point, tension developed in the co-supervision of a particular student. Evidently an expectation gap existed between us. It was not healthy and it was beginning to be quite obvious—even to our student leader. I attempted to move both strategically and indirectly. Diplomacy wasn't working. Encouragement and praise got me nowhere. Surprisingly, my charm didn't seem to be charming. Then I remembered those three simple words: "be disarmingly honest."

I set up a meeting with my colleague to talk about our co-supervision. When Michael came to my office I could literally feel the tension between us. I started like this: "Michael, let me be disarmingly honest. I have been able to tell for quite some time that there is tension here in our working relationship. Over the past few months, I have tried to figure out a way to make things better. I'm not sure if I did something to offend you, but if I have, I want to be able to talk through that. I feel like there is some animosity between us."

I won't say that the conversation was magical or that the heavens opened up and all was made right. I can't even say that our disarmingly honest conversation changed Michael's position. Something better happened. We clearly discussed the factors that made our working relationship so tedious for both of us. The disarmingly honest conversation created a space to express our frustrations, offer apologies and grant forgiveness, and to move forward in ways that led toward flourishing.

I expect that each of you is trying to strategically navigate a difficult relationship even now. I want to suggest that the best strategy is to introduce a disarmingly honest conversation.

There is no disarmingly honest conversation formula. It can look differently depending on you and your "Michael." But here are some steps I try to take:

> » I always open with a simple statement like: "I would like to have a disarmingly honest conversation. Would that be okay?" I have done this a lot. No one has yet to tell me it wasn't okay. Here's the point: it is disarmingly honest for a reason. When we approach someone with a humble posture and literally say that we want to clearly articulate something, it is truly disarming. It is disarming because it seldom happens. People generally want to know the truth. When it is prefaced with such a clear statement, one has a tendency to drop his guard and respond with his own disarming honesty.

> » Next, I explain how I perceive the state of affairs. Hopefully, by this point in your leadership, you have had the opportunity to learn some very basic communication skills when dealing with conflict. I like to tell my colleague or my student (or even my wife) how I see the

situation. Telling someone how things are is one of the best ways to move them toward defensive postures. Telling someone your perceptions or how things "seem" opens a dialogue. It communicates an understanding that you might just be wrong.

» I ask them, "Is this the way you see things?" Inviting their feedback to your assumptions is possibly the key to the conversation. Herein rests an invitation to reshape the story. Reality is always seen from different vantage points. And neither party has a God's-eye-view of the situation. The hope is to reorient perceptions—to make sense of the actions of both parties to the other.

» I always make sure that if there are missteps I have made or feelings I have hurt, I ask for forgiveness. Further, even if I don't agree with the person's perspective, I affirm them for sharing and thank them for their honesty.

» Knowing each other's assumptions, I ask, "How do you see us moving forward with this?" or "What if we tried this?"

» Most importantly, no matter how hard I want to, I don't try to win. Pride is the enemy of the disarmingly honest conversation. For the meeting to bear fruit, I need to set aside the desire to be right and work toward a mutually restorative way forward.

Michael was fresh out of college. Entering into a new position, he brought with him some views of how to work with undergraduate students that were different from my own. Thanks to the disarmingly honest conversation, I learned that my new colleague feared his loss of ownership and creativity in service to his residence hall. He feared that I would not allow him to work the way he saw fit. Ultimately, he wanted to establish his position.

As he spoke, I remembered feeling the exact same way in my early years at Penn State. Hearing his assumptions allowed me to empathize with his position. Although we didn't resolve the problems of the world that day—or even all of the issues of working together—we could move forward with a better understanding and more care for one another.

Being disarmingly honest is not only about conflict with others. It is also helpful as we consider asking for help or asking for others' perspectives. The conversation looks similar. This is related to our chapter on "Networking for the Common Good." Often times we don't ask for help on a project or for resources because we assume the answer will be no or that our request will seem presumptuous. Disarming honesty allows the person to decline while remaining open for them to say yes.

For me, it often starts like this: "Sharon, I am hesitant to ask because I know you have a busy schedule, but I was really hoping that you could speak on a panel about being a Christian in the workplace." Or perhaps, "Sam, I know budgets are really tight right now, but I have an idea for a program that I think could be really valuable. Is there any way to get funding for it?" This sort of disarmingly honest question acknowledges difficulties and helps to show that you are not being overly presumptuous.

In all of this, it is worth mentioning that disarmingly honest discourse must always be intended for the common good and established in love. The disarming honesty we suggest is never a blank check to say whatever you want. Nor is it permission to speak harmful words. Instead, it is always meant to draw to the surface the unspoken and often difficult things for the sake of restoration.

As we lead in a broken world, there is something about being disarmingly honest that is so very Kingdom oriented. Being disarmingly honest can lead us into restorative moments in relationships and will often open unexpected opportunities.

FOR DISCUSSION OR REFLECTION:

1. Have you ever encountered someone who was gifted in being disarmingly (and lovingly) honest? Talk about or reflect on that experience.

2. Think of a relationship or situation that could have been addressed with a disarmingly honest conversation. What did you do instead?

3. What is a circumstance you are currently in that could benefit from disarming honesty? Talk through or journal about how that conversation might proceed.

4. Are there times that don't call for disarmingly honest conversations? What might they be? How do you discern these?

PRACTICE:

1. During the week, reflect on a difficult situation you are currently in with a friend, a supervisor, or someone who is influenced by your leadership. Journal about your assumptions regarding the situation. Consider how they might see the situation differently.

2. Commit to having one disarmingly honest conversation this week. It might be something as simple as talking to a roommate about why they don't do the dishes. Then spend some time reflecting on how the conversation proceeded. What did you learn from it?

PRACTICE 5
Restorative Conflict

In the world of leadership, conflict will always be with you. It's not optional. Conflict in itself is unavoidable in the world of leading. The problem in life and leadership is conflict avoidance. Faithfulness is not measured by how little conflict we encounter, but rather by how we proceed in and through difficult situations. Conflict can take many shapes in your realm of influence. Whether dealing with issues stemming from personality differences, leadership perspectives, or prioritization, the following list provides guideposts for navigating difficult situations in leadership. Most of these approaches are profound in their simplicity.

GIVE THE BENEFIT OF THE DOUBT

When problems arise, whether it is interpersonal dynamics, disagreements on direction or strategies, or unmet expectations, the leader has two initial options: believe the best or assume the worst. I have experienced time and again that the initial human reaction is the latter. In a world distorted by sin, we do this all the time—before we ever ask questions or investigate the situation, we generally presume that the person has done something wrong and often with bad intent.

This is not usually the case. People make decisions (whether we agree with them or not) based on factors we do not see. When a team member doesn't show up for an important meeting, we assume that they forgot or blew it off. If we find out someone failed to complete a task, we consider it laziness or thoughtless disregard. This is the posture of the cynic. These things might be true—but often times there are additional factors that led to the issue.

When something goes wrong, before making judgments about another, ask questions to discern the actual state of affairs. Assuming the best until discovering otherwise, will keep conflicts from escalating and lead us into restored working relationships.

ADDRESS IMMEDIATELY

There is an old adage, "Time heals all wounds." Like many clichés, this is a lie. Think of the literal wounds our bodies suffer. We know by experience that a prescription of time is seldom the only thing called for. A nasty cut on your hand, left to itself, can fester with infection and even spread throughout the body causing irreparable harm. So it is with conflict. Time doesn't heal all wounds. Unaddressed conflict will also fester, sometimes below the surface, and spread throughout the community. The scriptures hold a better saying: "Do not let the sun go down on your anger" (Ephesians 4:26). It is given with a sense of urgency which is born of the reality of the human condition. We know this from the story. While it is appropriate to reflect on tension in leadership situations, circumstances must be dealt with swiftly, with care, and directly.

CONFLICT IN THE CONTEXT OF THE STORY

When I ask one of my friends how work is going, he often says with a smile, "It would be perfect if it weren't for all the humans." While this gets some easy laughs, it often feels so true. It is ironic that while we embrace the narrative of the scriptures that attest to the fact that we live and lead in a world of gravity and grace, of sin and redemption, we are often surprised when things get difficult. In chapter seven, we write at length about the reality of the world in which we lead and the effects of sin on that world. Although we do not want to embrace the posture of the cynic, we also should never be surprised by conflict in our realms of influence. It is going to happen.

IF YOU DON'T HAVE ANYTHING NICE TO SAY, SAY IT TO THEM

Naturally, many of these approaches to dealing with conflict or unmet expectations are interconnected at their root. One of the most insidious factors in the life of a community is gossip. It plagues the metaphorical water coolers of our world. Gossip disintegrates communities.

Here's a simple rule of thumb: If you don't have anything nice to say, say it to that person. This flows out of being direct and assuming the best. It also keeps us from talking (and more often complaining) about someone to others within our fields of influence.

The one caveat I will add is this: it is often very helpful to have one person that you can talk and reflect with about issues of tension. For me, at the college, it is Brian. I trust that I can share things with him and be able to use him as a sounding board. This trust emerges from years of relationship. We are good for each other this way, as we drive one another to follow each of the principles here. We can give advice on the best ways to proceed. Most often we help one another to develop perspective in difficult situations.

PRAY FOR YOUR ENEMIES

In the "Disarmingly Honest" chapter, I told the story of a difficult working relationship with my colleague Michael. The disagreements were driving both of us mad. Reading the scriptures one day, I was reminded of Jesus telling us to pray for our enemies. While I never really considered Michael an enemy, I was gripped by the serious tension between us. I committed to praying for him every day. These petitions were not focused on him seeing my perspective. In fact, I wasn't even praying about our working relationship. Instead, I prayed for Michael in all aspects of his life. I prayed for him and his girlfriend. I prayed for his work. I prayed that he would find joy in his hobbies and life outside of work. The result was profound. Slowly, day after day, I began to really care about him. Praying for our enemies and those with whom we have strife literally change our affection toward them. We begin to authentically want the best for them.

IT'S ALL IN THE FRUIT

To the Galatian church, Paul writes, "The fruit of the Spirit is love, joy, peace, patience, kindness, goodness, faithfulness, gentleness, self-control" (Galatians 5:22-23). These words are in response to what he calls the "works of the flesh." While several of these sinful works might seem far from our realms of influence (sorcery and orgies, I hope), most of them hit home: enmity, strife, jealousy, fits of anger, divisions, and envy. Any of these sound familiar? "The Fruit of the Spirit for the Leader" could be its own standalone book. Interestingly, the solution isn't a formula. The way beyond the insidious works of the flesh is through the Spirit. The Spirit of God, whom Jesus says is left as a helper, is the One who bears the fruit in us. What is the path to uncommon decency?[1] Bearing with one another and praying for the Spirit of God to fill us to the end of bearing fruit.

KNOW WHEN TO WALK AWAY

Sometime ago a colleague was attacked online by a blogger. The assault was directed at the content of his work and at his character. In response, our common friend stepped into the comment section and labored to argue for the sake of our mutual friend. He crafted lengthy arguments that were excellent in their rhetoric and content. In the end, it was as though he were talking to a wall. The blogger did not care to listen to winsome reason. Even as we approach conflict and difficult situations with care and love, sometimes things will not be resolved. The more that we care about restoration, the harder it is to know that there is a time to brush the dust from our sandals and walk away. At times this is necessary. Discernment, at times, calls for us to do this. Sadly, this side of the New Heavens and New Earth, resolution will not always happen. While we can still remain open to opportunities for reconciliation, there is a time—after attempting to deal with disagreement with care, prayer, and integrity—to walk away from a conflict.

FOR DISCUSSION OR REFLECTION:

1. Consider a conflict or tension you are a part of. What has led to this situation?

2. What assumptions do you hold about the other person? If you were to give the benefit of the doubt, how would those assumptions change?

3. How might you be "in the wrong"?

4. Discuss or reflect on ways you have seen gossip distort a community.

PRACTICE:

1. Spend time in prayer about a conflict with a coworker, supervisor, or friend. Commit to praying for their good every day. Pray for the Spirit to fill you and bear fruit.

2. Commit to honestly and directly addressing a conflict. Prayerfully approach this tension out of love for the other and for the sake of restoration.

PRACTICE 6
Rhythms of Rest

Leadership is tiring. Being an influencer in each of your spheres of life is a difficult journey. In this book we have looked at the challenge of faithfulness, the call to stewardship, and our roles as cultivators and restorers. These are just a few of the demands we each face. Leadership is not for the faint of heart. The good news is that it also comes with the directive to rest.

The scheduling patterns of our culture have created longer work weeks, shorter vacations, and very little time alone. Each week our calendars seem to turn into horrific vortexes as we try to fit everything in. We act as if busyness is next to godliness. We quickly forget that rhythms of rest were built into the creation from the very beginning. The Creator King took a day of rest to reflect on His creation, modeling the way to work. The author of Genesis tells us, "And on the seventh day God finished His work that He had done, and He rested on the seventh day from all His work that He had done. So God blessed the seventh day and made it holy, because on it God rested from all His work that He had done in creation" (Genesis 2:2-3). The

Sabbath was designated as holy. We also know that God prioritized rest by including it in the Ten Commandments. "Remember the Sabbath day, to keep it holy. Six days you shall labor, and do all your work, but the seventh day is a Sabbath to the LORD your God. On it you shall not do any work" (Exodus 20:8-10). The scriptures make it clear that rest must be part of the creation—even the land itself was given patterns of rest with the year of Jubilee.[1] Our leadership habits need to reflect these patterns.

Even with the clarity of these commands, we often neglect this area of our lives. This can be especially true for leaders with demanding schedules. We tend to ignore the importance of rest or feel trapped by the need to handle everything coming our way. It was not intended to be this way. Tim Keller writes:

> God liberated His people when they were slaves in Egypt, and in Deuteronomy 5:12–15, God ties the Sabbath to freedom from slavery. Anyone who over-works is really a slave. Anyone who cannot rest from work is a slave—to a need for success, to a materialistic culture, to exploitative employers, to parental expectations, or to all of the above. These slave masters will abuse you if you are not disciplined in the practice of Sabbath rest. Sabbath is a declaration of freedom.[2]

Stop being a slave to your schedule. Recognize the importance of rest. It is an essential aspect of leadership if you want to sustain your influence.

Creating rhythms of rest and intentional times of reflection must be a nonnegotiable practice in our lives. Finding times that allow you to reflect on God's goodness and to refresh your heart, soul, mind, and strength is crucial. An element of faithful stewardship is properly managing important resources. Time is one of those valuable resources. Here are some practices that may help you steward that resource.

DISCERN

Practicing rhythms of rest means first figuring out what should and should not be on our calendars. A colleague once told me that we are as busy as we want to be. This was a bizarre concept for me. I now realize that he was right. As stewards of our time, we make the decisions about what we do and don't do. Identify the pressures you feel in regards to your schedule, ask yourself where these are coming from.

Leaders, through the help of the Holy Spirit, must discern God's will for their lives and their leadership activities. This includes identifying which of those scheduling pressures should stay and which ones should go. Many leaders over the years have found the "Time Management Matrix," popularized by Stephen Covey, helpful when deciding what needs to happen with their time. It uses four quadrants to identify the importance and urgency of your tasks. Use this valuable resource as you plan for each week.

TAKE A SABBATH

It is worth restating the importance of Sabbath rest here. We were designed to operate with patterns of rest. And the key concept here is patterns—regular times of rest that are built into your schedule. It does very little good to only take a Sabbath after you have overdone yourself and cannot go on. Avoid these times of burnout by making rest a regular habit. This takes diligence. The commandment actually states that we labor for six days and rest on the seventh. Implied here is that we are getting our work done during those six days. It can be difficult, but build in nonnegotiable times of rest on a regular basis.

SAY NO

As a person of influence, you will be asked to do many things. Of course, as a person who longs to see good things accomplished in this world you will want to do many things. Learn to say no. It is an art and it takes practice. Learning to decline certain things that will not fit into the schedule is crucial. This may mean saying no to good things. These are difficult decisions, but you cannot say yes to every opportunity. It is helpful to have trusted people in your life to aid you in discerning which opportunities to say yes to and when to say no.

RECOGNIZE YOUR HUMANNESS

It is easier to say no to certain things when you are honest with yourself about being human. You cannot do it all. An important part of the fact that we are human is the responsibility to care for our bodies. Our bodies need rest, exercise, a balanced diet, and regular monitoring to stay fit and continue to function well. Remember that we all have possibilities and limitations. Leaders must learn to have a deep appreciation for this and maintain a healthy lifestyle.

PLAY

Work hard, play well. We must have a life that integrates playfulness with our workload. The Lord desires us to enjoy His creation and others in it. So play games that you enjoy, find a hobby that you like, spend regular time with friends, run in the rain, hike a quiet trail, immerse yourself in a novel, attend concerts. As leaders we often think that it is important to always be getting things done. Life is more than productivity, take time to play in the Kingdom.

CHOOSE HOPE

Leaders continually strive to take care of themselves. They understand that rest is invaluable. It is a practice that all leaders must embrace. Again, Tim Keller writes:

> The purpose of Sabbath is not simply to rejuvenate yourself in order to do more production, nor is it the pursuit of pleasure. The purpose of Sabbath is to enjoy your God, life in general, what you have accomplished in the world through His help, and the freedom you have in the gospel—the freedom from slavery to any material object or human expectation. The Sabbath is a sign of the hope that we have in the world to come.[3]

The practice of Sabbath allows us to continue choosing hope as we lead in a difficult and heavy world. Try these ideas that we have shared. Add others to the list that you find helpful. It will have significant impacts on your leadership.

FOR DISCUSSION OR REFLECTION:

1. Why is it difficult to take time to rest?

2. What are some practical ways you can enjoy the gift of rest?

3. What role does technology play in your life? Are there ways in which you should reconsider your use of technology in order to better practice restfulness?

PRACTICE:

1. Build into your schedule a time of rest. If you're not used to taking a Sabbath, try it out. Journal about changes you encounter. How does your attitude improve?

2. Make a list of non-negotiable calendar items and why you put them in this category.

3. Make a list of certain things you are going to stop doing. Ask someone to keep you accountable to this list.

Conclusion

Storied Leadership is a discovery and exploration of the foundations of leadership from a Christian perspective. The process of writing this book is, in a sense, a travel log for us—our own journal of reflecting on what the scriptures say about the world and our role in it, and with regards to leadership and influence. It has also been a process of new discovery, as we have continued to wrestle with the ideas explained here and the traditions from which they have emerged.

Drawing together the themes, we would like to offer what we consider five key "take aways" that we hope you will hold fast to as you complete your reading, reflection, and discussion:

> *All human activity emerges from a story depicting the way things are.*

The projects we commit ourselves to, the way we go about choosing a career, how we consider our interactions with others, where we shop, and yes, the way we lead and influence, are shaped by our fundamental belief commitments about the nature and state of the world. These are the questions concerning what humans are and their purposes in this world, and a vision of the future. All of this takes form in a narrative—a grand story that tells the tale of reality. There are many sources of story. Advertisers, the media, your friends, and your mentors are all living out of an account about the world we live in. Many of them are vying for your undivided attention—and some of them, by God's good grace, get aspects of the story right. Leadership from a Christian perspective requires a deep understanding of the biblical narrative from Creation to Revelation. On this foundation we are able to build a vibrant perspective of leading in a world of gravity and grace, of sin and restoration.

The Gospel is Cosmic.

The gospel has too often been reduced to the conception that Jesus died on the cross to save us as individuals from our sin. This leads to a mission that is reduced to sharing that gospel message with others. In and of itself, even this truncated gospel is very good news. However, we insist that the gospel is bigger. From the narrative in Genesis, we are entrusted with the world God has made and called to cultivate its potential into fullness. After the Fall, when all is distorted, we are commissioned to enact the work of making bent things straight. Paul, through his letter to the Colossians, instructs us that the work of Jesus Christ on the Cross is for the reconciliation of all things. We are His ambassadors of reconciliation. This good news is cosmic and affects all aspects of our lives. Who is a leader in the context of this big-picture gospel? He is one who leads people toward being creators, cultivators, and story-tellers. The call to leadership is not just for people who hold leadership positions. It is for each and every image bearer of the one true God. We are all called to work together for positive change.

Leadership is a tall order.

Considering the call to be a part of the nascent Kingdom that is at hand motivates us to work earnestly. Often times, when the time comes to get to work, to dirty our hands in the working in the world, we realize just how incredibly hard the calling before us is. People let us down, we make mistakes, funding falls through, and we realize that "the best laid plans of mice and men often go awry."[1] This is so true. Although it surprises us, it should not. Just as Adam, after the Fall, would work the land with sweat on his brow, so also we lead in a world filled with thorns and thistles. Leadership is hard. It will always be hard. The narrative of the story tells us it will be so. Yet, if we grasp the story in its fullness we expect this. Aware of the Fall, we understand that the things we do will not be the way they ought. The story dismantles the naiveté of the optimist. Knowing the story, we also realize that God's good grace is always active in our work as well. Friends, in the words of Garber, "make peace with the proximate." Remember that things will never be as they ought, but they will never be without glimmers of the grace of God. Holding fast to the proximate equips us to be neither naïve nor cynical as we lead toward a better world.

Leadership is a long journey.

The difficulty of leading in a broken world as broken people points toward faithfulness as pivotal in Kingdom leadership. Most are easily motivated around projects that are new, exciting, and even high-profile. As difficulties arise, when people are disinterested, or when you take on projects that are less than exciting, focusing on faithfulness is imperative. In the chapter on faithfulness, we draw on Eugene Peterson's conception of "a long obedience in the same direction." We encourage you to rethink the notion of long obedience. Our friend and mentor, Brad Frey, has lived out his passion for restorative work in our worn-down mill town for decades. Brad, a professor of sociology, has a vision for renewal in Beaver Falls. The work has been long and hard. Day after day, and year after year, Brad continues to work within institutions and alongside people in the hard calling to serve our city. Similarly, God has given you certain gifts and has placed you in a context within a particular community.

Kingdom leadership is faithful stewardship.

It includes much more than simply casting a vision and getting things done. Leadership is also about creating and cultivating, reconciling and restoring. This comes with an obligation of care. As a person of influence, you are charged with stewarding the gifts you are given, your relationships near and far, and the places entrusted to your care. God trusts us to pay attention to His creation and our responsibilities. With a clearer understanding of this you can consider each of your spheres of influence as an opportunity for stewardship. Continually identify these areas and evaluate their needs. This is what good caretakers do. Stewardship takes commitment; it is hardly quick and easy. It is essential, however, as you participate in the Kingdom story and lead for the common good

The second section of the book brought to the fore particular practices that we have found to be most significant in our own lives and leading over the years. Each emerges from our understanding of the story of the scriptures and applied to our own contemporary context. Although this book is primarily a work about building a foundation, we believe, in the end, that thoughtful, intentional practices that intersect with the real world and are mobilized for effective change are crucial. As you move forward, our deep hope is that the establishment of a groundwork for leadership will prove invaluable. We pray that a careful reading of the scriptures and their call toward the Kingdom of God will remain your foundation on which to work out faithful leadership. Remember, every practice emerges from a story about reality. The question is: What story is your leadership shaped by?

Amen.

Notes

ACKNOWLEDGMENTS
[1] Austin Kleon, *Steal Like an Artist* (New York: Workman Publishing, 2012), 11.

INTRODUCTION
[1] Daniel Muhlenburg, "Economists Explain Manhattan's Skyline for the First Time," *Elegran*, accessed October 2014, http://www.elegran.com/blog/2012/02/economists-explain-manhattans-skyline-for-the-first-time.
[2] Ralph Stodgill, *Handbook of Leadership: a Survey of Theory and Practice* (New York: Free Press, 1974), 259.
[3] Joseph C. Rost, *Leadership for the Twenty-First Century* (Westport: Praeger Publishers, 1993), 109.

CHAPTER 1
[1] Thomas Wolfe, *You Can't Go Home Again* (New York: Scribner, 1990), 628.
[2] Steven Bouma-Prediger and Brian J. Walsh, *Beyond Homelessness: Christian Faith in a Culture of Displacement* (Grand Rapids: Wm. B. Eerdmans Publishing, 2008), 13.

3 Craig G. Bartholomew and Michael W. Goheen, *Drama of Scripture: Finding Our Place in the Biblical Story* (Grand Rapids: Baker Academic, 2004), 18.

4 James K.A. Smith, *Desiring the Kingdom: Worship, Worldview, and Cultural Formation* (Grand Rapids: Baker Academic, 2009), 35.

5 Ibid, 108.

CHAPTER 2

1 To explore the philosophy of Dooyeweerd further, we recommend *The Dooyeweerd Pages*, found here: http://www.dooy.salford.ac.uk/ or the primer by J.M. Spier, *An Introduction to Christian Philosophy* (Ann Arbor: Craig Press, 1954).

2 I first heard this taught with wit and wisdom by Dr. Terry Thomas.

3 Emphasis mine.

CHAPTER 3

1 Wendell Berry, *The Art of the Commonplace: The Agrarian Essays of Wendell*, ed. Norman (Washington DC: Counterpoint, 2003), 186.

2 Ibid, 186.

3 Simone Weil, *Gravity and Grace*, trans. Arthur Wills (Lincoln: Bison Books, 1997).

CHAPTER 4

1 I am forever indebted to my mentor and friend, Dr. Donald Opitz. He helped me form much of my own teaching and living when it comes to leadership. I've used this phrase since the first time I heard him use it.

2 Gordon Spykman, *Reformational Theology: A New*

Paradigm for Doing Dogmatics (Grand Rapids, Mich.: W.B. Eerdmans Pub., 1992), 266.

3 Steven Garber, *Visions of Vocation: Common Grace for the Common Good* (Downer's Grove: InterVarsity Press, 2014), 180.

4 C. S. Lewis, *The Weight of Glory* (New York: HarperCollins, 1949), 163, 165.

5 As quoted in Wendy Jehanara Tremayne, *The Good Life Lab: Radical Experiments in Hands-On Living* (North Adams: Storey Publishing, 2013), 184.

6 As quoted in Lukman Harees, *Mirage of Dignity on the Highways of Human Progress: The Bystanders Perspective* (Bloomington: Authorhouse, 2012), 73.

7 Henry Cloud's Facebook page, accessed August 2014, https://www.facebook.com/DrHenryCloud/posts/10152201971784571.

8 Patrick Lencioni, *The Five Dysfunctions of a Team: A Leadership Fable* (San Francisco: Jossey-Bass, 2002), vii.

CHAPTER 5

1 Suzanne Collins, *The Hunger Games* (Danbury: Scholastic, 2009), 208.

2 Parker Palmer, *Let Your Life Speak: Listening for the Voice of Vocation* (San Francisco: Jossey-Bass, 2000), 88-89.

CHAPTER 6

1 This idea comes from author Andy Stanley, found in his book *The Next Generation Leader* (Colorado Springs: Multnomah Books, 2006).

2 James M. Kouzes and Barry Z. Posner, *The Leadership Challenge: How to Get Extraordinary Things Done in Organizations* (San Francisco: Jossey-Bass, 1987).

3 Max De Pree, *Leading without Power: Finding Hope in Serving Community* (San Francisco, Calif.: Jossey-Bass, 1997), 127.

4 Robert J. Banks and Kimberly Powell, *Faith in Leadership: How Leaders Live Out Their Faith in Their Work—and Why it Matters* (San Francisco: Jossey-Bass, 2000), 8.

5 It was an honor to spend time with David a couple times over the course of a year. His work is an inspiration to all. And he designed one of my favorite places in the world – PNC Park in Pittsburgh, PA. Check out the Convergence Design website at www.convergencedesignllc.com.

6 Henry Cloud, *Integrity: The Courage to Meet the Demands of Reality* (New York: Collins, 2006), 24.

7 Garber, *Visions*, 201.

8 Friedrich Wilhelm Nietzsche, *Beyond Good and Evil: Prelude to a Philosophy of the Future* (Cambridge: Cambridge University Press, 2002), chapter five.

9 Brian Jensen, adapted from "Beautifully Ordinary." Originally appeared on the site of The Washington Institute for Faith, Vocation, and Culture, July 2013, http://www.washingtoninst.org/5598/beautifully-ordinary/.

10 Many thanks to Paul Hurckman for introducing this concept to our work many years ago at North Central University.

11 We recognize that this concept caters to an idea of positional leadership. While it certainly helps provide a framework of understanding for positional leaders, it also helps us with an understanding of the power and responsibility of influence—something that all of us must grasp.

CHAPTER 7

[1] Garber, *Visions*, 220.

[2] For more on cynicism we recommend chapter 7 in Garber's *Visions of Vocation*.

[3] Peter Senge, *The Fifth Discipline: The Art and Practice of the Learning Organization* (New York: Crown Publishing Group, 2010), 135.

[4] Alain De Botton, *Status Anxiety* (New York: Knopf Doubleday Publishing Group, 2008), 119.

[5] J. R. R. Tolkien, *The Letters of JRR Tolkien,* eds. Humphrey Carpenter and Christopher Tolkien (New York: Harper Collins, 2010), 336.

[6] See Walter Brueggemann, *The Prophetic Imagination* (Minneapolis: Fortress Press, 2001), 39-42.

CHAPTER 8

[1] Palmer, *Let Your Life Speak*, 15.

[2] Much of this comes from Douglas Schuurman's book, *Vocation: Discerning Our Callings in Life* (Grand Rapids: Wm. B. Eerdmans Publishing, 2004). Check it out for a explanation of what a robust understanding of vocation looks like.

[3] James Davidson Hunter, *To Change the World: The Irony, Tragedy, and Possibility of Christianity in the Late Modern World* (New York: Oxford University Press, 2010), 252.

[4] Abraham Kuyper, *Lectures on Calvinism* (Grand Rapids: Eerdmans, 1931), 20.

[5] Thanks to Anjelica Farino. A student who is always sharing excellent insights with those around her.

[6] Eugene H. Peterson and Janice Stubbs Peterson, *Living*

the Message: Daily Help for Living the God-centered Life (San Francisco: Harper, 2002), 20.

[7] G.K Chesterton, *Othodoxy* (USA: Feather Trail, 2009), 42.

[8] James K.A. Smith, "Dream Small," *Comment*, accessed June 2014, http://www.cardus.ca/comment/article/2962/dream-small/.

PRACTICE 2

[1] Keith Ferrazzi, *Never Eat Alone: And Other Secrets to Success, One Relationship at a Time* (New York: Crown Business, 2005).

PRACTICE 3

[1] Andy Stanley, Catalyst Conference, Atlanta, GA, October 2009.

PRACTICE 5

[1] For a book that explores living and interacting in a community of difference, we recommend Richard Mouw, *Uncommon Decency: Christian Civility in an Uncivil World* (Downers Grove: InterVarsity Press, 2010).

PRACTICE 6

[1] See Leviticus chapter 25 for a Biblical understanding of this concept that was woven into the Creation design.

[2] Timothy Keller, "Wisdom of Sabbath Rest," *Q Ideas*, accessed June 2014, http://qideas.org/articles/wisdom-and-sabbath-rest/.

[3] Ibid.

CONCLUSION

[1] While often attributed to John Steinbeck, this is a

common paraphrase of a line from Robert Burn's 1785 poem "To a Mouse."

About the Authors

Brian Jensen is Dean of Student Development at Geneva College where he has also served as faculty in Humanities and Leadership. He holds a BS in Business Administration from North Central University and an MA in Higher Education from Geneva College. Brian lives in Beaver Falls with his wife Sara and kids Levi, Toby, and Zoe.

Contact Brian at:
bcjens@gmail.com or @StoriedLeader on Twitter

Keith R Martel is Associate Professor of Higher Education and also serves as faculty in Political Science at Geneva College. He is currently the director of the Master of Arts in Higher Education program. He holds a BA in Political Science and Philosophy and an MA in Higher Education from Geneva College, and a PhD in Philosophy from Duquesne University. Keith lives in Beaver Falls with his wife Kristie, kids Gavin and Simone, and dog Echo.

Contact Keith at:
krmartel@gmail.com or @krmartel on Twitter

41015297R00121

Made in the USA
Charleston, SC
20 April 2015